Life a

Life along the Border

A LANDMARK TEJANA THESIS

By Jovita González

Edited, with an Introduction, by
María Eugenia Cotera

TEXAS A&M UNIVERSITY PRESS
College Station

The paper used in this book meets the minimum requirements
of the American National Standard for Permanence
of Paper for Printed Library Materials, z39.48-1984.
Binding materials have been chosen for durability.

The photograph of Jovita González on p. 36 is courtesy of the
E. E. Mireles and Jovita González Mireles Papers,
Special Collections and Archives, Mary and Jeff Bell Library,
Texas A&M University–Corpus Christi.

LIBRARY OF CONGRESS CATALOGING-IN-PUBLICATION DATA

Mireles, Jovita González, 1904–1983.
 Life along the border : a landmark tejana thesis / by Jovita González ;
edited, with an introduction, by María Eugenia Cotera.— 1st ed.
  p. cm. — (Elma Dill Russell Spencer series in the West and
Southwest ; no. 26)
 Includes bibliographical references and index.
 ISBN-13: 978-1-58544-521-9 (cloth : alk. paper)
 ISBN-10: 1-58544-521-5 (cloth : alk. paper)
 ISBN-13: 978-1-58544-564-6 (pbk. : alk. paper)
 ISBN-10: 1-58544-564-9 (pbk. : alk. paper)
  1. Cameron County (Tex.)—Social life and customs. 2. Starr County
(Tex.)—Social life and customs. 3. Zapata County (Tex.)—Social life and
customs. 4. Cameron County (Tex.)—History, Local. 5. Starr County (Tex.)—
History, Local. 6. Zapata County (Tex.)—History, Local. 7. Mexican
Americans—Texas, South—Social life and customs. 8. Mexican Americans—
Texas, South—History. 9. Texas—Relations—Mexico. 10. Mexico—
Relations—Texas. I. Cotera, Maria Eugenia, 1964- II. Title. III. Series.
 F392.C25M57 2006
 976.4'495—dc22   2006005126

Contents

Preface

Jovita González's master's thesis, "Social Life in Cameron, Starr, and Zapata Counties," has, for most of its life in the world of letters, remained chastely cloistered in a few libraries scattered across the Southwest. This truly unfortunate circumstance, which the current volume seeks to remedy, has prevented generations of scholars from experiencing the full depth and breadth of our collective intellectual history. The text is now presented here in its entirety, with minimal extra-textual commentary and an introduction that helps to establish the historical context in which it was written. A few editorial changes have been made to the format of the thesis to ensure that it conforms to current scholarly conventions, but otherwise the text is as it appeared when Jovita González first submitted it to her thesis advisor, Eugene C. Barker, in 1930.

"Social Life in Cameron, Starr, and Zapata Counties," is a social history of the borderlands written by one of its "native daughters." As such it offers a picture of the place and its people that could only have come from the mind of a woman on the border between epochs, races, languages, and cultures. Such a woman was Jovita González, who, despite an array of forces marshaled against her—economic, social, patriarchal—managed to articulate a unique vision of the history of her people. This vision, laid out in the following pages, has lingered for far too many years in near-obscurity, relegated to the margins of academic inquiry in footnotes, microfilm, and the storage facilities of major research libraries.

It is a vision that would likely never have seen publication were it not for the dedication of my mentor and friend Dr. José Limón, who first brought the work of Jovita González to my attention. Indeed, it was Limón who introduced González to a whole generation of scholars through his recovery and publication of two of her manuscripts: *Dew on the Thorn,* a book-length folklore study she wrote in the mid-1930s, published in 1997 by Arte Publico Press; and *Caballero,* a historical novel she coauthored with an Anglo woman, Margaret Eimer, in the late 1930s, published in 1996 by Texas A&M University Press. Both of these works have brought much-needed attention to this previously overlooked and underrated scholar and have helped to burnish her reputation as an astute observer of the Latina/o condition. I thank Dr. Limón for his efforts to enrich our collective knowledge of Jovita González's work, and I hope that the present volume will contribute to our deepening understanding of both Jovita González and her generation.

—*María Eugenia Cotera*
University of Michigan

PART I

Introduction

A Woman of the Borderlands

✻

"Social Life in Cameron, Starr, and Zapata Counties" and the Origins of Borderlands Discourse

MARÍA EUGENIA COTERA

"A text," observes intellectual historian Dominick La Capra, is an "event in the history of language." This succinct assessment of the relationship between language, history, and texts cuts two ways. On the one hand it revivifies texts by suggesting that they are much more than dead words on paper, that they have a kind of life, an active quality that has the power—like all "events"—to shape history. On the other hand, La Capra's formulation points to the historicity of language itself; the words we speak, how we choose to use them, their very meanings, represent the residue of an extended dialectical struggle over the uses of language. Language, after all, is both the primary vehicle, and, as La Capra suggests, the primary terrain, through which the interventions of public intellectuals are expressed. I am drawn to La Capra's formulation not least because it allows me to think about our shared intellectual history and to chart the ways, both various and subtle, that scholars who have come before me have used texts to wage battle.

For some time now, I have been pondering the complicated intellectual legacy of Jovita González, a (relatively) celebrated folklorist who circulated in the milieu of the mostly white, primarily male Texas Folklore Society of the 1920s and 1930s. González, a Mexican American woman, was immersed in this milieu during a period in which Texas history was undergoing a "whitewashing" of sorts: when scholars like folklorist J. Frank Dobie and historians Eugene Barker and Walter Prescott Webb were producing popular books that—for the most part—functioned as nostalgic apologias for Anglo imperialism. The writers of this period, more than any others, are responsible for structuring the very language of Texas history that Chicano scholars simultaneously inherited and disavowed in the 1960s. Indeed, Chicana literary critic Leticia Garza Falcón has argued that the language employed by Barker, Webb, Dobie, and others to describe and define Texas history and culture constituted a "rhetoric of dominance" that made the exclusion and domination of Mexicans and Indians seem natural and even justified.[1] So just what was Jovita González, daughter of the borderlands, doing hanging out with these rhetoriticians of dominance? More importantly, what was the nature of her political and institutional relationship with these men? Did she acquiesce to their vision of Texas history and culture? Did she provide a kind of multicultural cover for what was essentially a discourse designed to disenfranchise?

There is a kind of dominant narrative about Jovita González's interactions with the founding fathers of Texas history and folklore studies. The narrative goes something like this: Jovita González, daughter of the old (*Tejano*) order, collaborated with the sons of the new (Anglo) order, but did so with a degree of ambivalence that complicates the generally nostalgic tone of her folklore work. Folklorist and literary critic José Limón has artfully explored this complex terrain in *Dancing with the Devil,* drawing out the moments of contradiction and even resistance in Jovita González's writing and in her public performances at Texas Folklore Society meetings. Limón takes us back to a turning point in young Jovita González's career as a professional folklorist, speculating on her inner thoughts as she gave her very first presentation to the Texas Folklore Society in 1927. "Let us imagine her," he begins,

> Standing there on a podium on a stage. In southern Texas, in 1927, the war continues as Mexican agricultural strikes are violently suppressed, . . . but here, at this academic meeting, do not her delightfully accented words flow like soothing balm to the gathered company of mostly white men—some of them rich, powerful men? In his customary cowboy boots, his Stetson hat politely in his lap, does her Don Pancho [J. Frank Dobie] sit there also, probably in the first row? Dare we hope that as she read her paper, she at least thought to herself of the "fatalistic" Catarino Garza who shot it out with Captain Bourke? . . . We dare hope, but it is only hope.[2]

Wishful thinking aside, Jose Limón's examination of Gonzalez's folklore work offers a nuanced and thought-provoking reading of González as a "native intellectual" engaged in a necessarily covert "war of position" within the institutional matrix of the Texas Folklore Society. But what if this war of position was not quite as covert as we all have imagined? What if González *did* imagine herself shooting it out with Captain Bourke (or perhaps one of his descendants)—not with a pistol in her hand, but a pen?

In 1930, just a few years after the presentation that Limón so evocatively describes, Jovita González wrote a master's thesis on the social history of the U.S.-Mexico borderlands and submitted it to historian Eugene C. Barker. It is to this "event" in the contested history of language about Texas that I now wish to turn, because I believe that her thesis, innocuously titled "Social Life in Cameron, Starr, and Zapata Counties," represents an extended and quite open argument against the rhetoric of dominance that was at the time of its writing consolidating itself in the discourse of the very figures to whom she presented her work. This astonishing fact, that a Mexican American woman in 1930 would have thought it reasonable to submit for review a piece of work that contested the very foundational fictions upon which Texas historians were building a seemingly unassailable edifice, is worth noting, especially since so much of the conventional wisdom about González figures her as a benign collaborator with power. The question at the heart of this introduction is then, if "Social Life in Cameron, Starr, and Zapata Counties" is an "event" in the history of language about Mexicans and Anglos in the making of Texas, then just what sort of event is it?

TO LIVE IN THE BORDERLANDS MEANS YOU . . .

Before we can fully comprehend both the courage that it took to write "Social Life in Cameron, Starr, and Zapata Counties" and the impact that the thesis must have had on her Anglo colleagues at the University of Texas, we must know something of the author herself. What took her from the remote terrain of the U.S.-Mexico borderlands to the relatively cosmopolitan domain of Austin and the University of Texas? Why did she pursue—against all odds—a career in folklore, an emerging field of disciplinary knowledge populated for the most part by colorfully garrulous Anglo men and genteel Anglo ladies whose vision of Texas culture and history was often clouded by romantic notions regarding its nonwhite inhabitants? And why, just two years into her career as a folklorist, did she choose to take time out to write a master's thesis on the social history of the borderlands when she could just as well have continued on what was an undeniably successful professional trajectory?

Jovita González was born near the Texas-Mexico border on January 18, 1904. Her father, a native of Mexico, came from a family of "educators and artisans," but her mother's family had a much older provenance in Texas. They had owned land on both sides of the border for over five generations, and, according to González, her maternal grandparents were direct descendants of the colonizers who had established the first settlements in Nuevo Santander under the leadership of Don José Escandón. Notwithstanding their instrumental role in the colonization of the region, Jovita González's ancestors were forced to flee from Texas shortly after the Treaty of Guadalupe was signed in 1848 ending hostilities between Mexico and the United States. The family reestablished itself in Texas after the Civil War, when González's grandfather—with financial support from his widowed mother, Ramona Guerra Hinojosa (González's beloved "Mamá Ramoncita")—was able to repurchase some of the land that was lost after 1848. On this land, located in Starr County near Roma, Texas, he established "Las Viboras," the ranch where González was born.

González's early life was filled with stories and legends from the people who lived and worked in and around her grandfather's *rancho*. In her memoirs, she vividly recalls scenes and people from her childhood, many of which reappear in her later writing. González remembers her Tia Lola with special fondness. Tia Lola was her mother's sister who came to live with them at Las Viboras as a young widow. It was the strong-willed Tia Lola who taught González and her siblings about their family's heritage in Texas, and, González implies, it was Tia Lola who ensured that their early education was rounded out with plenty of information about important women in history. As young girls, Jovita and her sister Tula memorized a poem in Spanish entitled "La Influencia de la Mujer" (The Influence of a Woman) that charted a distinctly feminist historical heritage, beginning with "Judith, the Old Testament heroine," and ending with "Doña Josefa Ortíz de Dominguez, the Mother of Mexico's Independence." The girls also learned about Sor Juana Ines de la Cruz, and were familiar with her famous feminist poem "Hombres Necios" (Foolish Men).

Despite the nostalgic tone of her reminiscences, the years that González and her family spent at Las Viboras were not easy ones for Mexicans in South Texas. Indeed, the year of Jovita González's birth also marked a turning point in the economic and political destiny of the border communities. On July 4, 1904, the rail line from Corpus Christi to Brownsville was completed. Financed largely by Anglo ranchers and businessmen, the *Saint Louis, Brownsville, and Mexico Railway* finally connected Corpus Christi (and the Missouri-Pacific railroad system) to Brownsville, opening up the Valley to massive land speculation. The establishment of the railroad brought South Texas firmly into the fold of the market economy of the United States. As historian David Montejano notes, "With the railroad came farmers, and behind them came land developers, irrigation engineers, and northern produce brokers. By 1907, the three-year-old railway was hauling about five hundred carloads of farm products from the Valley."[3]

The railway was also hauling hundreds of midwesterners into the region, lured by the age-old promise of westward expansion, seeking to rebuild their lives in what was promoted as the "Magic Valley." These Anglo immigrants brought with them not only the hope for a new start in an unexploited territory but also a poisonous racial ideology that was often at odds with that of the established Anglo-Mexican ranching community. Despite the hostility between Anglos and Mexicans that necessarily accompanied the U.S.-Mexico War in 1848, in the years that followed, relations between Anglos and Mexicans in the border region soon normalized due to the small Anglo population and the region's isolation from the world beyond the Nueces River. Intermarriage between Anglo military men and entrepreneurs and the daughters of landed families was a fairly regular occurrence, and many of these men adopted the religion, language, and social customs of their wives. However, the new racial order that accompanied massive Anglo emigration to the area supplanted these relatively accommodative race relations with segregationist "Jim Crow" policies that regulated interracial contact, and created a caste-like system that separated Mexicans and Anglos in a variety of social spheres ranging from the educational system to public spaces like theaters and beaches.[4]

While Anglo-Mexican relations in South Texas had always been shot through with conflict regarding race and nationality, the type of "race thinking" that was at the root of the segregationist policies of the new social order represented a particularly pernicious amalgam of imported and indigenous racialist ideologies. The anti-Mexican sentiments generated by the bitter experiences of the War for Texas Independence in 1836 and the U.S.-Mexico War in 1848 were now bolstered by popular eugenicist and Anglo-Saxon theories of racial difference. Montejano notes that the distinct brand of "race thinking" that emerged in South Texas during the boom years was a pastiche of Western, Southern, and Eastern racialist ideology: "Texan history and folklore, previous experience with other races, biological and medical theories, Anglo-Saxon nationalism—all furnished important themes for farm settlers in their dealings with Mexicans." Whether these racialist ideologies were "indigenous or imported in content," they contributed to a "culture of race thinking that made the segregated world a reasonable and natural order."[5]

After the entry of the railroad and the attendant agricultural "boom," it became clear to Texas Mexicans that social, political, and economic relations in South Texas would never be the same. Indeed, the agrarian development of the Valley signaled the final blow to the remnants of Mexican hegemony in the region, and, according to Montejano, it further "eroded the centuries-old class structure of the Mexican ranch settlements." Within fifteen years of the construction of the railway system, the Texas Mexican people of the border region, with a few exceptions, were reduced to the "status of landless and dependent wage laborers."[6] In the end, the modernization process that brought South Texas into the national and international flow of goods and services led to the demise of the world that Jovita González knew, "the world of cattle *hacendados* [ranchmen] and *vaqueros* [cowboys]," and eventually led to the rise of "a world of commercial farmers and migrant laborers." By the mid 1920s, horses and carts had been replaced by automobiles and highways; and segregated public parks, movie houses, and drugstores took precedence over the plazas, churches, and *haciendas* (ranches) as places to meet and exchange news.[7]

AN EDUCATION IN EXILE

In her memoirs, González recounts that her family moved away from the border region in 1910 so that she and her siblings might receive an "education in English," but there can be little doubt that the need for a more standardized education was overshadowed by the dramatic economic and cultural changes taking place in the borderlands during this period. The Mexican Revolution kept border communities in constant turmoil. Moreover, racial terror against Mexican Americans was on an upsurge, propelled by an increasingly militant response to the Anglo invasion on the part of Mexican Americans who had been left behind by the economic "boom."[8] Despite the worsening conditions for *Mexicanos* in South Texas, things could not have been much better in San Antonio, where Anglos had come to dominate political and economic life some fifty years earlier. In the outline notes to her memoirs, González includes the phrase "some unpleasant incidents" in the section dealing with her early years in San Antonio. In the final draft of her memoirs no mention of these "unpleasant incidents" is made, but it is easy to imagine how difficult it must have been for a young Texas Mexican girl from the borderlands to adjust to the new racial order of Anglo-dominated San Antonio. Nevertheless, González persevered in the face of culture shock and her lack of English proficiency. Thanks to the informal ranch-house schooling in English that she received at Las Viboras and her somewhat more thorough education in Spanish, González was able to advance to the fourth grade by the age of ten and, by attending school in the summer, finish her high school equivalency by the age of eighteen.

González's somewhat circuitous path through higher education in the early 1920s is testament to the financial and institutional barriers limiting the professional aspirations of Mexican American women of her generation. Though the pursuit of a university education was always a given for her, González lacked financial resources of her own to support such an endeavor and thus was under constant pressure to earn enough money to pay for her education. Her family's shaky financial situation only compounded these difficulties. González's educational career is thus marked by interruptions caused either by her own lack of funds to continue her schooling or by the need to dedicate what little funds she did have to the support of her family. Upon graduation from high school, González decided to return to the borderlands to work as a teacher in order to earn money for her college fund. She enrolled in a Summer Normal School earning a teaching certificate in two years, and then returned to South Texas to take on a teaching position in Río Grande City where she lived with her aunt and uncle. This arrangement allowed her to save up enough money to enroll at the University of Texas in the fall.

After finishing her freshman year in Spanish, González was forced to return to her parents' home in San Antonio because of lack of funds. Again she turned to teaching to raise money, this time in Encinal, Texas, where she served as head teacher of a small two-teacher school. After two years of teaching, González decided to return to college, though not to the University of Texas. She enrolled in summer school at Our Lady of the Lake College in San Antonio, where she was offered a scholarship for the following year in exchange for her services as a Spanish teacher in its affiliated high school. The deal was too good to pass up: "For teaching two hours a day and a class of teachers on Saturday, I would get a private room, board, and tuition. My worries were over." Despite this ideal situation, González yearned to return to the University of Texas where she had begun studies in "advanced Spanish" under Lilia Casis a few years earlier, "Once having her as a teacher I could not consider anyone else."[9] So González added yet another job to her already cramped schedule: She began tutoring fellow students at Our Lady of the Lake College in order to earn enough money to enroll for summer school at the University of Texas.

Gonzalez's hard work eventually paid off. In the summer of 1925, her mentor Lilia Casis introduced her to J. Frank Dobie, the celebrated professor of English who had put Texas folklore studies on the map. This introduction was a turning point in Jovita González's life. "Heretofore," she recalled, "the legends and stories of the border were interesting, so I thought, just to me. However, he made me see their importance and encouraged me to write them, which I did, publishing some in the Folk-Lore Publications and Southwest Review."[10] González is far too modest in this account. The story of her involvement with J. Frank Dobie and the Texas Folklore Society is certainly much more complicated than this. Indeed, this fateful meeting had far-reaching implications for the ways in which the dialogue over Texas culture and history would be played out over the rest of the century.

ROMANCING THE BORDER: JOVITA GONZÁLEZ
AND THE TEXAS FOLKLORE SOCIETY

When Jovita González discovered folklore studies in the late 1920s, she found a congenial community of scholars who were consumed by the giddy possibilities that popular interest in regional folklore had created. These were "boom years" for Texas folklore studies; with public interest in regional traditions at an all time high, the Texas chapter of the American Folklore Society was leading the way in the movement to popularize the study of "the folk." The Texas Folklore Society owed much of its success to the vision of J. Frank Dobie, the man who would become Jovita González's mentor in the field. Dobie was a humanist (his master's degree was in English), and as such he was less interested in the scientific categorization of different folk artifacts (tales, songs, games) than he was in the utility of folk material to contemporary culture. He proposed the collection of the folklore of "the four peoples that have mingled their lore in the Southwest" (the "Anglo-Saxon," the "Negro," the "Indian" and the "Spanish"), hoping that the legends and lore of these rural folk communities might inspire modern authors to explore regional themes in their writing, much in the same way that the legends of New York State had inspired Washington Irving to create the first home-grown literary movement in the United States.[11] Essentially, Dobie envisioned folklore as the raw material for the development of a uniquely American—and uniquely regional—literary form.

Dobie's romantic investment in the folk and folklore of his region, and his antipathy to more scientific approaches to folklore studies not only reflected the general aesthetic values of his period but also his personal background. A native son of the Anglo ranching community, Dobie was fascinated by what he believed was a "vanishing" way of life. As a young adult (Dobie was born in 1888) he witnessed the wave of agricultural development that had consumed the open ranges of his childhood and transformed formerly sleepy Texas towns into booming mercantile centers. Like González, Dobie recognized that the rugged ranch life that characterized his informal education was quickly disappearing. His experiences as a young man working on his uncle's ranch in South Texas also reinforced a deep and abiding respect for the largely dispossessed Texas-Mexican *vaqueros* who worked the ranch. However, about Mexicans Dobie was ultimately ambivalent: on the one hand, because he had grown up on a ranch worked almost entirely by Mexicans, he idolized *vaqueros* for their simplicity, their nearness to the land, and their unabashed masculinity; on the other hand, he was a son of the Anglo ranching elite, the very community that had (often violently) dispossessed the "freedom loving *vaquero*."[12]

Dobie's contradictory nostalgia structured the pursuit of knowledge about the Mexican folk in Texas for over thirty years. Under his direction, the Texas Folklore Society turned increasingly to the collection of the folklore of the dispossessed with special attention to the folk traditions of Mexicans in Texas. However, their renditions of folklore tended toward the ahistorical and apolitical—focusing, for example, on plant and animal lore, *curanderismo* (folk healing), and legends of lost treasure—the forms of cultural poetics that, in Dobie's estimation, offered his general readership the true "flavor" of the folk. Thus, while Dobie's focus on Mexican folklore traditions during this period did promote general interest in Mexican culture, it rarely moved beyond the "appreciation" of Mexican arts, crafts, and narrative traditions. As a result, while the "beauty" of Mexican culture was often celebrated, the political and social valences at the heart of Mexican cultural poetics in Texas were left largely unexplored. As folklore historian James Charles McNutt observes, "Beyond the purpose of collecting and presenting the materials for literary use, there was little conscious attention to the question of what folklore was supposed to mean for the people whose spirit it presumably expressed."[13]

In spite of the contradictions at the center of its formation—or perhaps because of them—the brand of romantic folklore studies that Dobie promoted at the University of Texas in the 1920s and 1930s did initiate "a liberating exploration of the boundaries which separated the various 'folk' of the Southwest." And even though the Texas Folklore Society generally "kept racial and ethnic conflict conveniently in the romantic past," the very process of exploring culture across ethnic and racial lines brought increasing interaction between these groups and a new-found respect for the cultural poetics of Mexican Americans in Texas. Indeed, the methodological innovations that Dobie and his cohorts brought to the study of the folk in Texas and the Southwest permanently transformed the political and aesthetic landscape of regional folklore studies. Because Dobie and his liberal Anglo colleagues promoted "a limited but important encouragement of collection by non-Anglo folklorists," they ushered in a period of unprecedented dialogue between Anglo and "ethnic" public intellectuals.[14] For the first time in the tradition of knowledge production about culture and history in Texas, Mexicans were a part of the conversation, and a new generation of Mexican American scholars entered into this dialogue. People like Carlos E. Castañeda, Lilia Casis, and Jovita González played instrumental roles in the organizational structure of the Texas Folklore Society, and contributed significantly to the production of knowledge about their communities. Moreover, the flexibility that Dobie built into the research methodologies of the organization enabled a greater number of non-professional Mexican American folklorists (like Adina de Zavala) to collect material on the folk practices of their neighborhoods, towns, and ranches.

For Dobie, Jovita González embodied the virtues of the ideal collector of folklore. Her fine literary abilities in combination with her "authentic" insider knowledge of the intimate customs of ranch life granted her a certain degree of ethnographic authority within the field of Texas folklore studies. On the occasion of her first contribution to the *Publications of the Texas Folklore Society* (*PTFS*), an article entitled "Folklore of the Texas-Mexican Vaquero" (1927), Dobie played up González's personal history, noting somewhat hyperbolically that: "Her great-grandfather was the richest land owner of the Texas border. . . . Thus she has an unusual heritage of intimacy with her subject."[15] Dobie clearly believed that his readers would appreciate González's contributions more if they knew that she represented an "authentic" folk subject, someone who had actually lived among the *rancheros* and *vaqueros* of South Texas. In fact, González's "authenticity" as a daughter of *ranchero* culture constituted the very foundation of her ethnographic authority, and she was not beyond capitalizing on this patina of authenticity to further her own position within the world of folklore studies at the University of Texas. For Dobie, Jovita González might have represented a more "safe" and "sanitized" version of his idealized *vaquero*. As an educated daughter of the *ranchero* elite, she was removed from the more violent contradictions of Anglo/Mexican ranching culture on at least two levels: her gender relegated her to the feminized domestic world of the *rancho*, the world of plant-lore, legends, and folk remedies; and her presumably "elite" status brought her in line with Dobie's own ideological vision. But González refused to remain within the cloistered walls of the hacienda. Her first contributions to the *PTFS* focused on the songs and legends of the masculine world of the *vaqueros*, and though, as José Limón has noted, she sometimes adopted the "superior, often condescending and stereotyping colonialist tone" of her mentor in these articles, "it is an idiom that at times appears to be repressing a certain sense of admiration for these classes and an acknowledgment of the state of war." Indeed, in his analysis of González's early folklore studies, Jose Limón has expertly uncovered "key instances of a counter-competing vision on questions of race, class, and gender domination."[16] There are other indications that in spite of their friendly relationship, González did not always agree with Dobie's (and, by extension, the Texas Folklore Society's) version of Texas history. In a 1981 interview with James Charles McNutt, González revealed that she avoided Dobie's classes because the two shared such disparate views on Texas history: "You see, it was an agreement that we made, that I would not go into one of his classes because I would be mad at many things. He would take the Anglo-Saxon side naturally. I would take the Spanish and Mexican side." González acknowledged that many of her Mexican colleagues at the University of Texas were also careful not to contest the "official history" promoted by Dobie and his cohort: "teachers couldn't afford to get involved in a controversy between Mexico and the University of Texas . . . if the history of Texas were written the way it actually was . . . because things, some of those things that happened on both sides were very bitter. So we just didn't mention them. You just forget about it."[17] González's comments graphically illustrate the limitations she experienced in speaking for the "Mexican side" in the public dialogue over Texas history.

However, there is at least one instance during this period when Jovita González did insert her voice rather forcefully into this public dialogue. In 1929, just two years after completing her bachelor's degree at Our Lady of the Lake, González was granted a Lapham Scholarship to take time off from teaching and conduct research along the border in order to complete her master's degree at the University of Texas. González spent the summer of 1929 traveling through South Texas collecting notes for what would become perhaps her most vocal native-born critique of ethnographic, sociological, and historical representations of Mexicans in Texas, her master's thesis, "Social Life in Cameron, Starr, and Zapata Counties."

SOCIAL LIFE IN CAMERON, STARR, AND ZAPATA COUNTIES: A CRITIQUE FROM THE BORDERLANDS

Although she is best known as an expert in the field of folklore, when Jovita González decided to pursue an advanced degree she did so in history under the guidance of Eugene C. Barker. While we may never know the reason she decided to get a master's degree in history as opposed to English (where she would have studied under her mentor, J. Frank Dobie) or in Spanish (under Lilia Casis), we do know that Barker was singularly unenthusiastic about the thesis González submitted to him for approval in 1930.[18] Indeed, he was initially reluctant to approve her thesis, and may not have done so had it not been for the intercession of her old friend Carlos Castañeda.[19]

As González recalls in her memoirs, though Barker found the thesis "interesting," he also thought it "somewhat odd"; which is not surprising since, in both form and content, it subverts many of the norms of western and southwestern historiography that he had helped to establish. Indeed, though they were both key players in the study of Texas culture and history, Barker and González clearly embodied radically different visions of Texas history. In his lectures and in his books, Barker placed the Texas Revolution (1836) at the veritable center of Texas history, as a kind of foundational moment of national formation. Writing from the perspective of the borderlands, González saw the Texas Revolution as merely one instance in the long history of transnational conflict that plagued the region.[20] For González, the "foundational moment" for Texas came almost a century before the Texas Revolution, with the founding of the first permanent Spanish settlements just north of the Río Grande. Gonzalez's refusal to follow the accepted storyline of Texas history—especially her rejection of the Texas Revolution as a foundational moment in Texas history—placed her at odds with the version of history popularized by Barker, Walter Prescott Webb, and even J. Frank Dobie. It also suggests a subtle claim for the historical legitimacy of the region's Mexican inhabitants. For González the "founding fathers" of Texas were not the heroes of the Texas Revolution—Austin, Bowie, Houston—but the *Criollo* and *Mestizo* heads of families who established ranches along the Río Grande in the eighteenth century. Her recovery of the story of their settlement of South Texas establishes the rootedness of Mexicans in Texas and thus counteracts the "rhetoric of dominance" that sought to make them invisible.

Essentially what Jovita González presented to Eugene C. Barker in 1930 was a counter-history, a narrative that offered a Mexican perspective on the history of Texas and contested negative representation of *Mexicano* culture and people, which might explain both her decision to take on the field of history for her thesis work and Barker's initial reluctance to approve the final results of her research. Indeed, although he claimed that the thesis lacked sufficient "historical references," Barker may well have been more alarmed by the strident counter discursive tone of González's account of "social life" on the Texas-Mexico border. This tone, forcefully forecasted in the author's introduction, clearly represented a departure from "business as usual" in Texas history circles. One need only note how González begins her thesis to see why Barker may have thought it "somewhat odd."

There exists in Texas a common tendency among Anglo-Americans, particularly among Americans of one or two generations' stay in the country, to look down upon the Mexicans of the border counties as interlopers, undesirable aliens, and a menace to the community. Those among the last group named who have this opinion should before making a definite stand consider the following: First, that the majority of these so-called undesirable aliens have been in the state long before Texas was Texas; second, that these people were here long before these new Americans crowded the deck of the immigrant ship; third, that a great number of the Mexican people in the border did not come as immigrants, but are the descendants of the *agraciados* who held grants from the Spanish crown.[21]

In this introductory statement, González neatly reverses the racialist discourse that had come to dominate both popular and scholarly representations of Texas history and culture, reminding her readers that not all Mexicans are immigrants, and that most Anglo-Americans come from immigrant stock themselves.[22] Keeping with the spirit of this opening salvo, González proceeds to offer a counter-history of Texas that begins with its settlement by Spanish and Mexican colonizers in the eighteenth century and then moves on to an account of nineteenth-century Texas that seems scarcely recognizable to those of us raised on Davy Crockett and the "heroes of the Alamo." Indeed, in González's version of Texas history the Texas Revolution and the U.S.-Mexico War fade into relative obscurity, and become simply two more examples in a long history of "border troubles" whose origins were essentially transnational in nature. Her analysis of the too-often overlooked Wars of Federation (1839) and the Carbajal Rebellion (1851) not only enrich the historical panorama of the region, they also help to reframe the borderlands as a transnational zone in which the political machinations of central Mexico have as much impact as those in Austin or Washington, D.C. Moreover, by demonstrating the many instances in which *Tejano* attempts to create bicultural political coalitions with Anglo settlers against the *centralista* government in Mexico City were undermined by Anglo political machinations and greed, González enacts a subtle but devastating critique of dominant narratives about the "founding fathers" of Texas. In effect, she recasts the "heroes" of Texas—from the politicians to the "freebooters" and the "entrepreneurs"—not as defenders of freedom against Mexican despotism, but as despoilers of legitimate democratic movements (led by idealistic *Tejanos*). Her account of nineteenth-century border struggles in Texas thus reverses the heroic narrative that had come to dominate both popular and scholarly accounts of Texas history—a narrative that cast the forces of progress and democracy (embodied in "freedom-loving" Anglos) against the forces of despotism (embodied in the villainous figure of Mexico's president, Santa Ana) by offering a more complex and multidimensional vision of historical events in which "heroism" and "villainy" are not the sole property of any one nation or race.

González carries this complex and multidimensional vision of border conflict into her discussion of social banditry, deploying it to deconstruct what had become a common trope of the Anglo new order in its justification for racial repression: the claim that Mexicans were inherently "lawless." As Gonzalez astutely argues, the "lawlessness" of the border must be understood within the larger context of American imperialism and economic expansion.

Mexicans considered the Americans in Texas as interlopers, no less than vandals, who had by deception and intrigue deprived them of one of their states. They looked indiscriminately upon all Americans as aggressors, waiting to deprive them of their personal possessions as they had deprived the mother country of a whole province. On the other hand, the Americans looked upon the Mexicans as a conquered, inferior race, despised because of their ability to check American advances. Because they were the conquered race, the Mexicans were considered cowards and everything that was low and despicable.

Everything a Mexican did was wrong. During a period of lawlessness when both Mexican and American ranchmen stole freely from each other, the former paid the greater price. Whether Mexicans or Texans originated this illegal exchange of cattle is unknown, but the fact remains that it existed and that its existence led to many abuses and much bloodshed. While the big ranchmen prospered and profited, the small

Texas-Mexican landowner was forced to abandon his property and either become a peón or leave the country . . . As a natural result, frictions were constant along the border.[23]

In a strategic re-reading of banditry as the natural result of the political and economic after-effects of American imperial expansion, González explodes the assumption that lawlessness is always and only connected to individual economic imperatives. In her view, such acts are at once economic and nationalistic: a mode of resisting imperialist forces, and a mode of protecting one's "personal possessions." Moreover, by asserting that, "both Mexican and American ranchmen stole freely from each other," while conquered Mexican *rancheros* "paid the greater price," González pointedly implies that the American legal system, ostensibly the objective source of "justice" in the United States, ultimately served the economic interests of Anglo ranchmen. What emerges in this discussion is, then, a fundamental reevaluation of the concept of "theft" in which the *real* thieves are those "interlopers" who by "deception and intrigue" dispossessed Mexico of "a whole province," and who later dispossessed Mexicans of their land and resources through the manipulation of a biased legal system. González cleverly reforms Mexican "bandits" by presenting them as "small Texas-Mexican landowners" protecting both national honor and property rights from "vandals" in the form of "big ranchmen" and systemic corruption. What is made clear in González's account of the history of conflict in the borderlands is that one's view of "history" depends upon which side of the border one occupies. By radically decentering the accepted narrative of "Texas History," González reveals the perspectival nature of historiography itself.

This complex and multidimensional perspective is also evident in González's assessment of the political, social, and cultural life of *Tejanos* on the border both before and after the "invasion of fortune-seeking Americans."[24] Here, González offers a picture of a culture group in transition, whose traditions, language, and social conventions are tested and transformed by the twin historical forces of modernization and contact with Anglo-American culture. But unlike Américo Paredes, her most famous successor in the contested world of Texas folklore studies, Jovita González does not present the *Tejano* community of the nineteenth century as some prelapsarian utopia. Instead, she offers an unflinching examination of the oppressive ideologies and social contradictions that fractured the *Tejano* community along race, gender, and class lines *before* the influx of Anglos and the agricultural "boom."

In his classic treatise on Texas-Mexican resistance, *With His Pistol in His Hand*, Paredes proposes an undeniably romantic reading of nineteenth century South Texas as a premodern class utopia in which *peón*, *vaquero*, and *ranchero* coexist in relative harmony.

The simple pastoral life led by most Border people fostered a natural equality among men. Much has been written about the democratizing influence of a horse culture. More important was the fact that on the Border the landowner lived and worked upon his land. There was almost no gap between the owner and his cowhand, who often was related to him anyway. The simplicity of the life led by both employer and employee also helped make them feel that they were not different kinds of men, even if one was richer than the other. . . .

The peón was usually a *fuereño*, an "outsider" from central Mexico, but on the border he was not a serf. Peón in Nuevo Santander had preserved much of its old meaning of "man on foot." The gap between the peón and the vaquero was not extreme, though the man on horseback had a job with more prestige, one which was considered to involve more danger and more skill.

The peón, however, could and did rise in the social scale. People along the Border who like to remember genealogies and study family trees can tell of instances in which a man came to the Border as a peón . . . and ended his life as a vaquero, while his son began life as a vaquero and ended it as a small landowner, and the grandson married into the old family that had employed his—the whole process taking place before the Madero revolution.[25]

González's perspective on the social stratifications that divided Border communities before the Mexican Revolution is somewhat less sanguine. She describes a social order in which the *ranchero* acted as "feudal lord" in a patriarchal system, wielding total power over his land, women, and *peónes*. González explains that like the Southern slave economy, the economic success of the *rancho* was grounded on a debt-peonage system that extracted profit from the forced labor of all but enslaved subjects. This debt peonage system, transplanted from northern Mexico, had, according to González, created subjects without a "will."

> An unfortunate situation resulted from this system, it gave the master absolute power over the *peón*, and this control converted him into a machine whom the landlord could work at his will. The *peón* realizing his position grew pessimistic and developed a spirit of hopelessness and despair. There was no incentive for him to save, since whatever he might save by economizing went to the landlord. The master exercised complete control over the *peón*, economically and socially as well as in religious matters.[26]

González's picture of life on the *rancho* deviates from Paredes's in at least one other significant way: it includes a gendered critique of the patriarchal order. An undeniably elegiac masculine tone suffuses Paredes's depiction of ranch life—his descriptions are replete with uncritical evocations of patriarchal power, the rights of primogeniture, and a distinctly male-centered code of honor. In contrast, González casts a critical eye on patriarchal culture in "Social Life in Cameron, Starr, and Zapata Counties," carefully delineating the gendered contradictions of the *ranchero* worldview.

> A man was expected to have his escapades, in fact the more conquests, the more of a Don Juan he was, the greater the glory to his name. But woe to the woman, wife, daughter, or sister, who dared by her actions to besmirch family honor. An action which in a man was overlooked as insignificant was an unpardonable

offense for a woman. As the depository of family honor, woman was always under the direct rule of man. When she married she passed from her father's dominion to that of her husband's. As in most Spanish countries, her position was a contradiction. She had complete control in the home management, yet she lived a life of conventual seclusion. Married at an early age, and not for love, but for family connections and considerations, she made a submissive wife and an excellent mother.[27]

González does not limit her treatment of gender to the occasional critique of patriarchy; she also spends a good deal of time taking the reader through the social spaces and gendered practices in which the often invisible expressions of women's work and women's thinking are found. Her descriptive forays into the artfulness of altar-building, the education of young women, traditional domestic and religious practices, and the interior decoration of *ranchos* give us a picture of gendered forms of social interaction that greatly expands our understanding of the social world of the *rancho*. Indeed, González's description of ranch life stands in stark contrast to that of Paredes, who focuses on the exclusively male domain of "horse culture."

Contemporary critics might argue that Paredes was merely reflecting the gendered assumptions of his time in these evocations, but this is only partially true. The masculinist utopia evoked in the first few pages of *With His Pistol in His Hand* serves an important rhetorical purpose: it adds a heroic dimension to what is essentially a counter-hegemonic reading of social banditry. It is the very foundation upon which Paredes's narrative of loss, resistance, and revenge is built. González, on the other hand, either cannot or will not invoke the heroic past in her narrative of loss and resistance. Instead she offers a perhaps less satisfying but more realistic vision of the borderlands as a geopolitical zone rife with conflict and contradiction with respect to both its less-than-utopic past and its future possibilities.

In this section of González's thesis—her musings on the future of the *Mexicano* community—scholars of the Mexican American experience will find the most valuable information. González's final chapters,

"Border Politics" and "What the Coming of the Americans Has Meant to the Border People" include extensive interviews with both older *Mexicanos* who witnessed the transition from the old social order to the new, and "the younger generation," an emergent educated and professional class who, in González's words, embodied a veritable "renaissance in the Border." In these chapters, González cites from her interviews at length, allowing her informants to voice a narrative of transition, loss, and transformation that highlights the darker side of the agricultural boom period in South Texas. Her informants poignantly express their sense of anger, defeat, and humiliation at the rise of a new social and economic order that lumped land-owning classes of *Mexicanos* together with laborers and newly arrived Mexican immigrants in a bifurcated racial system whose only distinctions were between "white" and "non-white." These interviews offer a native-born perspective on the knotted racial logic of whiteness that was consistently invoked to exile Mexicans (whatever their class) from social spaces that had once been their exclusive domain.

But this is no simple tragic narrative of loss at the hands of an invading economic, political, and cultural force. Here too, González complicates the picture, suggesting that the Mexican elite felt the transition from old order to new most keenly, primarily because they had the most to lose. González points out that it was the "old families" who resented "the gulf with which the newly arrived Americans have separated them" the most. "Not that they are anxious for the friendship of the American families but they object to the fact that they are considered an inferior race. The word *white*, which the Americans use to differentiate themselves from the Mexican population, is like a red flag to a bull."[28] However, she also argues that the economic changes that came with the agriculture boom actually improved the status of the "*jornalero*" or "day laborer" class. For this working class population, the rise of a new ruling elite:

> [M]eant more than a change of masters, it meant more work, better wages, and improved living conditions. No class of society has gained as much by the economic changes as the *jornalero* class has. As previously stated, there has been a shifting of the

day laborers from the ranches to the cities. And this has been a great step in the improvement of their condition. However hard their work may be in the towns, it is not as heavy as what they had to do on the ranches, and the wages are much better. Whereas they had earned fifty cents a day as farm hands or goat herds, they are making now anywhere from one dollar to two dollars per day. The old one room *jacal* [shack] has been replaced by a small lumber house for which they are paying on the installment plan. The laborers themselves are better dressed, they wear store-bought clothes and their wives may attain their highest ambition, wearing a hat. . . .The children of this class are doing something that their parents never accomplished; they are going to school, learning to read, to write, and to speak English. Altogether, they are thoroughly satisfied with their lot.[29]

In these passages González demonstrates that class interests do not always coincide with race solidarity even in times of war. As she astutely points out, for the *Mexicano* working-class who had occupied the bottom of a highly stratified social system for generations, "the difference between them and their [Anglo] masters [was] no greater than that which separated them from their former *amos* [masters]."[30]

There are indications toward the end of "Social Life in Cameron, Starr, and Zapata Counties" that González viewed the transformation of the borderlands at the dawn of the twentieth century as a crucible upon which a new kind of identity was being formed—an identity located at the intersection of cultures, languages, and nations. Here, the tragic narrative of loss voiced by the older generation butts up against the somewhat less bleak and certainly more pragmatic vision of a younger generation who, for González, represented a "renaissance in the borderlands." González quotes one "young married man" from Hidalgo County at length, allowing him to map out his twentieth century solution to the "inter-racial problem."

It is our place and our duty now to learn American ways, to send our children to American schools, to learn the English language, not that we are ashamed of our Mexican descent, but because these things will enable us to demand our rights and to improve ourselves. We understand our race, and when we are able to comprehend American ideas and ideals, American ways and customs, we shall be worth twice as much as they, and we certainly shall have the advantage over them. Americans are egoists, and provincial, they over estimate their power and doing so are unwilling to see any other way but their own. It is to our advantage then, to educate ourselves in American institutions, to learn the English language and to exercise our rights as citizens. My children are to receive a public education here, and when they graduate, I shall send them to Mexico for at least two years in order that they may perfect themselves in the Spanish language and that they may know Mexico as Mexico is. We are going now through a very painful period of transition and like the white black bird do not know yet just what we are. Mexicans from across the river look down upon us and call us by what to them is the vilest epithet, *Texanos* and the Americans do not consider us as such, although some of our Texas-Mexican families have lived here for generations.

For years we have been part of a big political machine, our vote has not been individual, but now that we are becoming conscious of the meaning of citizenship we want to exert our privileges as individuals. Our labor is arduous, the future welfare of the Texas-Mexicans depends on what will be accomplished during this generation.[31]

Reviled by *Mexicanos* in Mexico for being a "*Texano*," rejected by "Americans" in the United States for being "Mexican," this *Mexican American* understands all too clearly that he and his generation must make the most of their "in-between" status. His proposal is to take the linguistic, cultural, and political traditions of both cultures and use them to benefit an emergent Mexican American community.

In a masterful, rhetorical stroke, Jovita González employs this interview to put a human face on the political discourse of the "League of United Latin American Citizens," an organization founded in Corpus Christi, Texas, in 1929. González touches on the emergence of LULAC and its political significance in South Texas in her "Border Politics" chapter, citing their founding document verbatim. Her analysis of LULAC is notable for a number of reasons. First of all, it represents one of the earliest assessments of this organization by a Mexican American scholar.[32] As such, it offers contemporary scholars of the Mexican American experience a unique opportunity to "witness" the founding moment of this organization through the highly critical eyes of a Mexican American intellectual of the time. And González's views on LULAC are quite interesting. Neither celebratory nor entirely dismissive, she contextualizes the founding of LULAC within a troubled history of border politics that included the rise of Anglo and Mexican political fiefdoms, their frequent disenfranchisement of working-class Mexicanos, bloody electoral battles, and, not surprisingly, extreme "political apathy" among the Mexican American electorate. According to González, LULAC was founded through a new kind of alliance between the leaders of the old ranchero families and the "newly created urban middle class" who, "conscious of the needs of their less fortunate fellow citizens, want to bring them out of the political apathy to which they have succumbed."[33] González clearly sees the goals of LULAC as a political embodiment of a new kind of borderlands subject who (like the "young married man" she interviewed in Hidalgo county) understands the importance of maintaining certain cultural traditions but also acknowledges the importance of adopting Anglo political, economic, and cultural tools in order to deal with the new reality in the borderlands. Notwithstanding her association of LULAC with some of the more hopeful transformations happening in the borderlands, González sounds a note of wariness in her evaluation of LULAC's male leadership. "One thing is characteristic of all these men," González warns, "[t]hey are politicians, and that is where the danger lies. Border politics are just emerging from political bossism and rings. If the League tends to educate the Mexican Americans for purely altruistic reasons, its labor no doubt is meritorious and praiseworthy. But should county bossism be superseded by an organized state wide political machine, the results will be detrimental not only to the Mexican American citizens but to the state at large."[34]

González's wariness regarding the political motivations behind LU-
LAC's powerful male leadership signals a highly sophisticated understanding of Mexican American political discourse in Texas. While she
sensed that the LULAC's ideological cocktail of "respect for cultural traditions" and celebration of progressive "American" civic principles could
offer a way out from under the oppressive racial system that had politically marginalized Mexicans in Texas, she was also clear-eyed about the
leadership's strong ties to "political bosses" of the old social order. As
such, she suspected that LULAC might be used to create a vast political machine that would merely perpetuate the disenfranchisement of
working-class Texas Mexicans. Moreover, her repeated invocation of the
leadership's *maleness* subtly points to the unstated gender biases of the
organization, which from its inception in 1929 until well into the 1960s,
maintained a gender-segregated organizational structure, limiting wom-
en's participation to auxiliary "councils" known as "Ladies LULAC."[35]

González's foray into the founding of LULAC in her chapter on
"Border Politics" brings up an interesting issue with respect to her
thesis in general: why is it that so much of this *history* thesis is dedicated to events on the border circa 1929? Indeed, according to folklore historian James Charles McNutt, Barker's reluctance to approve
González's thesis was due in part to her rather generous definition of
"Texas history," which included an examination of contemporary race
relations in South Texas. McNutt notes that while Barker "appreci-
ated her discussion of land grants," he objected "when she launched
into the social history of the descendants of the grantees."[36] Contemporary Chicana/o scholars may find themselves at odds with Barker's
evaluation on this score. While González's historical research on
Spanish land grants and her ethno-historical examination of nineteenth-century border life are certainly useful, the most riveting information offered in her thesis comes in those final chapters that include interviews with subjects who are deeply resentful of the rise of
Anglo-American political and economic hegemony in the region.

Perhaps González's ultimate aim was to set the historical record
straight as to the Mexican legacy in Texas, and then allow her informants to voice resistance to their continuing erasure under the discursive force of the "rhetoric of dominance" embodied in the work

of more established historians of the American West. In this respect, "Social Life in Cameron, Starr, and Zapata Counties," demonstrates that González was acutely aware of the power of discourse to control and determine the lives of its subjects. As Chicano historian David Gutierrez has noted, "Military conquest or absorption of one society by another usually represents only the first step of the process by which one society imposes itself on another. Ultimately, however, the most crucial development as a result of expansion and domination is the subsequent construction of an elaborate set of rationales which are designed to explain why one group has conquered another." González's effort to intervene against this second *discursive* phase of colonial domination is testament to Gutierrez's observation that "a substantial portion of the ethnic conflict that has occurred historically in the American West has involved subject peoples' efforts to contest and resist efforts to impose ascriptive social judgments on them, particularly by interpreting and representing their histories in certain ways."[37]

But Jovita González's early attempt to "contest and resist" dominant representations of border culture and history is important to scholars of the Mexican American experience for at least two other reasons. First, it potentially reframes our understanding of her intellectual and political engagement with the Texas Folklore Society and its "rhetoriticians of dominance." Scholarly assessments of González's folklore writing have generally gravitated between readings of her ideology as either "accomodationist" or, in the best case, as engaging in a form of muted resistance. The tenor and narrative structure of this, her earliest lengthy analysis of the border and its people suggests a much more oppositional and resistant subject. More intriguingly, "Social Life in Cameron, Starr, and Zapata Counties" offers a vision of the borderlands that seems deeply familiar to contemporary readers of borderlands discourse. Indeed, though its rhetorical thrust is undeniably counter-discursive, González's thesis moves beyond an agonistic rewriting of Texas history to highlight the complexities and contradictions of border culture both before and after the "invasion" of Anglo-Americans. For González, the "border" was clearly something more complex than a simple geopolitical dividing line between two nations and cultures, it was a contact zone where multiple cultures, languages, and histories—Indian, Spanish, Mexican, Anglo—had collided and recombined, forming a distinct and categorically different kind of regional identity, a borderlands identity. "Social Life in Cameron, Starr, and Zapata Counties" offers an unusually "contemporary" vision of the borderlands that documents the emergence of this identity, an identity that González herself—as a woman on the border—embodied. Indeed, if as Dominick la Capra suggests, Jovita González's thesis is an "event" in the history of language, it might be fruitfully thought of as an *introduction*.

NOTES TO INTRODUCTION

1. Leticia M. Garza-Falcón, *Gente Decente: A Borderlands Response to the Rhetoric of Dominance* (Austin: University of Texas Press, 1998).

2. José E. Limón, *Dancing with the Devil: Society and Cultural Poetics in Mexican-American South Texas* (Madison: University of Wisconsin Press, 1994), 64–65.

3. David Montejano, *Anglos and Mexicans in the Making of Texas, 1836–1986* (Austin: University of Texas Press, 1987), 107. For more on the unique form of racial apartheid that developed in South Texas in the early twentieth century see: Neil Foley, *The White Scourge: Mexicans, Blacks, and Poor Whites in Texas Cotton Culture* (Berkeley: University of California Press, 1997); and Benjamin Heber Johnson, *Revolution in Texas: How a Forgotten Rebellion and Its Bloody Suppression Turned Mexicans into Americans* (New Haven: Yale University Press, 2003).

4. Jovita González, "Social Life in Cameron, Starr, and Zapata Counties" (master's thesis, University of Texas, 1930), 110–13.

5. Montejano, 161.

6. Ibid., 114.

7. Ibid., 161.

8. The growing antagonism between Anglos and Mexicans in South Texas culminated in a homegrown insurrection. In 1915, a group of Mexican Americans drafted "El Plan de San Diego" a broadside calling for citizens of Mexican, Indian, Black, and Japanese descent to form a "Liberating Army for Races and People" in an effort to combat "Yankee tyranny." The rebellion was squashed, with brutal force, by the Texas

Rangers in 1917. For more information on El Plan de San Diego and its political and economic impact on South Texas see Montejano, *Anglos and Mexicans*, 117–25; and Johnson, *Revolution in Texas*, passim.

9. Jovita González, "Early Life and Education" in *Dew on the Thorn*, ed. José Limón (Houston: Arte Público Press, 1997), xii.

10. Ibid., xii.

11. Roger Abrahams and Richard Bauman, "Doing Folklore Texas Style," in *"And Other Neighborly Names": Social Process and Cultural Image in Texas Folklore*, ed. Richard Bauman and Roger D. Abrahams (Austin: University of Texas Press, 1981), 4–5. For more on Washington Irving and the "The Knickerbocker Group," the literary movement he inspired, see: James W. Tuttleton, ed., *Washington Irving: The Critical Reaction* (New York: AMS Press, 1993); and Ralph M. Aderman, ed., *Critical Essays on Washington Irving* (Boston, Mass.: G. K. Hall, 1990).

12. Dobie speaks fondly and quite eloquently of this youthful education in the legends and songs of *vaqueros* in his preface to *Tongues of the Monte*, first published in 1935. See J. Frank Dobie, "Preface: The Trail to Mexico," in *Tongues of the Monte* (Austin: University of Texas Press, 1987), passim.

13. James Charles McNutt, *Beyond Regionalism: Texas Folklorists and the Emergence of a Post-Regional Consciousness* (Ph.D. diss., University of Texas, 1982 [Ann Arbor: UMI, 1997. 8513331]), text-fiche, 235.

14. Ibid., 226.

15. J. Frank Dobie, ed., *Texas and Southwestern Lore*, Publications of the Texas Folklore Society VI (Austin: Texas Folklore Society, 1927), 241.

16. José E. Limón, *Dancing with the Devil: Society and Cultural Poetics in Mexican-American South Texas* (Madison: University of Wisconsin Press, 1994), 62.

17. McNutt, 350–51.

18. González may well have chosen to write her master's thesis in history at the urging of family friend, Carlos E. Castañeda who was a close colleague of Barker's. Or perhaps her choice represented a disciplinary rejection of the ahistorical and highly romanticized vision of the *Tejano* folk promoted by J. Frank Dobie in the English Department.

19. Carlos Castañeda insisted to Barker that González's thesis would be used as source material for years to come. Castañeda's prediction was

prescient, "Social Life in Cameron, Starr, and Zapata Counties" *has* been used as source material by generations of Chicano scholars including Américo Paredes, David Montejano, Arnoldo de León, and Benjamin Johnson.

20. A celebrated historian of the Texas Revolution, Eugene C. Barker had written a biography of Stephen F. Austin, whom he considered to be the "founding father" of Texas. He had also recently published his popular lecture series on Texas/Mexico political relations and the causes of the Texas Revolution. Jovita González must have been well acquainted with Barker's version of Texas history since he was her thesis advisor and they had been circulating in the same scholarly circles for at least two years. And Barker must certainly have realized that this was no ordinary master's student. Within the small enclave of Texas folklore and history enthusiasts, Jovita González was becoming a celebrity in her own right. She was already the vice-president of the Texas Folklore Society and was about to assume its presidency. And she was gaining a reputation beyond the confines of the University of Texas: "Folklore of the Texas-Mexican Vaquero," her contribution to the 1927 TFS Publication *Texas and South-western Lore* was singled out as the "best piece in the collection" in the *New York Times Review of Books* (November 13, 1927).

21. González, "Social Life," 41.

22. The narrative structure of González's thesis, specifically the elements of the thesis that focus on the daily activities and religious practices of border people in the nineteenth century, mirrors that of the earliest ethno-historical representation of the Texas-Mexicans, "The American Congo" (1894), a xenophobic tract written by ethnologist and U.S. military agent John Gregory Bourke. In fact, much of "Social Life in Cameron, Starr, and Zapata Counties" is quite literally *dialogic*, in that it addresses, point by point, Bourke's representation of border culture, strategically re-writing his imperialist ruminations on the people and culture of the Texas Mexican border. For a detailed analysis of the dialogic nature of González's thesis, see María Cotera, "Refiguring the 'American Congo': Jovita González, John Gregory Bourke and the Battle over Ethnohistorical Representations of the Borderlands," in "Recovering a Mexican-American West," special issue, *Western American Literature* 35.1 (2000).

23. González, "Social Life," 52.

24. González, "Social Life," 110.

25. Américo Paredes, *With His Pistol in His Hand: A Border Ballad and Its Hero* (Austin: University of Texas Press, 1958), 10–11.

26. González, "Social Life," 77.

27. Ibid., 81.

28. Ibid., 112.

29. Ibid., 110–11.

30. Ibid., 111.

31. Ibid., 113–14.

32. The first article written on LULAC was a glowing endorsement written by sociologist Douglas Weeks. González pulls the list of LULAC's twenty-five "Aims and Purposes" directly from Weeks' article though she may also have had access to LULAC's earliest documents through family friends, many of whom were active in Mexican-American politics at the time. See O. Douglas Weeks, "The League of United Latin American Citizens," *The South-Western Political and Social Science Quarterly*, repr., X, no. 3 (December, 1929): 257–78.

33. González, "Social Life," 104.

34. Ibid., 108.

35. For more information on LULAC's gender politics see Cynthia E. Orozco, "The Origins of the League of United Latin American Citizens (LULAC) and the Mexican American Civil Rights Movement in Texas with an Analysis of Women's Participation in a Gendered Context, 1910–1929" (Ph.D. diss., University of California, 1992).

36. McNutt, 251.

37. David Gutierrez, "Significant to Whom? Mexican Americans and the History of the American West," *Western Historical Quarterly* 24.4 (November 1993): 520.

PART II

*Social Life in Cameron, Starr,
and Zapata Counties*

THE MASTER'S THESIS
OF JOVITA GONZÁLEZ

Social Life
in Cameron, Starr,
and Zapata Counties

THESIS

Presented to the Faculty
of the Graduate School of The University of Texas
in Partial Fulfillment of the Requirements

For the Degree of
Master of the Arts

By

Jovita González
(San Antonio, Texas)
Austin, Texas
August, 1930

PREFACE

Thanks are extended to Dr. Eugene C. Barker for his patient guidance in directing the work of this thesis, to Mrs. Mattie Austin Hatcher, Miss Winnie Allen, of the Library of the University of Texas, and to Mr. C. E. Castañeda of the García Collection for assistance in locating source material for this work. Special thanks are also due the good border people who so willingly allowed the writer to interview them on many occasions.

INTRODUCTION

There exists in Texas a common tendency among Anglo-Americans, particularly among Americans of one or two generations' stay in the country, to look down upon the Mexicans of the border counties as interlopers, undesirable aliens, and a menace to the community. Those among the last group named who have this opinion should before making a definite stand consider the following: First, that the majority of these so-called undesirable aliens have been in the state long before Texas was Texas; second, that these people were here long before these new Americans crowded the deck of the immigrant ship; third, that a great number of the Mexican people in the border did not come as immigrants, but are the descendants of the *agraciados* who held grants from the Spanish crown.

The work here presented is not intended to be a glorification of the Texas-Mexicans. It is merely a historical and social study of a people, who, although forming a part of the United States, live apart from the rest of the country, following their own racial customs and traditions.

The historical material had been gathered from sources at the Library of the University of Texas. The description of social life is based primarily upon study and observation of the communities described. It concerns the Mexican population of the border counties where now live the descendants of the original grantees.

People in all social spheres were interviewed, politicians, bankers, ranchmen, and laborers, and their ideas together with the impressions of the writer have been combined particularly in the last chapter of this thesis.

With the hope that a better understanding between the two races will soon prevail in the border communities, this thesis is presented.

CHAPTER 1
Historical Background

CHAPTER 2
History of the Settlements at Zapata, Roma, Río Grande City, and Brownsville

CHAPTER 3
Present Mexican Population in the Counties Considered

CHAPTER 4
Social and Economic Life before the Development of the Lower Río Grande Valley

CHAPTER 5
Border Politics

CHAPTER 6
What the Coming of the Americans Has Meant to the Border People

CHAPTER I

Historical Background

The northern movement of Spanish explorations and settlements made the region between the Panuco and the Nueces rivers a place of refuge for the Indian tribes that were driven out by this expansion. These bands, broken down in numbers but not in spirit, became the scourge of the settlers in the northern frontier of New Spain. A pioneer Indian fighter and frontiersman, Barbadillo, was commissioned by the Spanish government to lead a punitive expedition into the Karankawa country in 1715. His work was effective only while he remained in the country; the dispersion of the Indian tribes and their segregation into missions came to naught with his removal from the region. No sooner had he been recalled than the country was again the prey of Indian attacks. The government in New Spain then realized that the only means of securing this land for the crown was by the establishment of permanent settlements in the region east of the territory known as the Huasteca and north of Nuevo León.[1]

To facilitate the organization of this Indian infested country, it was created into a new province—Nuevo Santander. With the approval of the Auditor General de Guerra, the Marquis of Altamira, and the consent of Revilla Gigedo, then viceroy, the reduction, or the conquest, of the newly created province was entrusted to Don José Escandón, a man of military experience and executive ability.

In 1748 Escandón left San Luis Potosi for Nuevo Santander with a force of 7,500 men and a colonizing contingent of 2,500 settlers composed of Spaniards and converted Indians. Efficient and thorough in the work assigned him, he had two purposes in mind; namely, the exploration of the Nueces and the Río Grande region, and the location of suitable sites for settlements along these streams. Prior to this expedition in the years 1746 and 1747 he had explored the first, and as a result of this had recommended the foundation of fourteen villas and a suitable number of missions.[2]

This colonizing movement interested not only those who were concerned officially, but also the ranchmen and stockmen who were desirous of extending their grazing lands northward beyond the Río Grande. These frontier cattlemen, with the approval of Escandón, were instrumental in founding the towns and villas along the Río Grande, which were later to form the nucleus of the Hispanic-Mexican migration into Texas.

While in the Río Grande River region, Escandón founded several missions and towns along the coast and hills of Tamaulipas. Knowing of this and of his proposed plan to found others, which would strengthen the claims to the newly created province, Don Vicente Guerra, a native of Coahuila, asked permission to found a villa on the Salado River. The territory in question was already claimed by Guerra, who had established ranches on it some years before. He proposed to bring without cost to the royal treasury, and at his own expense, the necessary number of families to found the proposed town, adding that he would also cede part of his own land to the colony provided it were held in common. For all these favors to the crown he asked to be made captain and administrator of the colony. Escandón accepted this advantageous proposal, and as a result Revilla, now Guerrero, was founded October 10, 1750, with families from Coahuila and Nuevo León.

Later Don José Baez Benavides and his five brothers offered Escandón their cooperation in furthering the progress of the community if he would give them definite possession of the territory on which they had established their ranches. Escandón gave his consent, and on the death of the captain at Revilla, Benavides was named to succeed him.[3]

At the same time that Revilla was founded, Don José Vasquez Borrego, a rich ranchman from Coahuila, crossed the river into what is now Texas and established himself at a place called Dolores. Like Guerra and Benavides, he offered Escandón his help and cooperation in the enterprise of pacifying the country, and like the others [he] was named captain and administrator of the settlement.

The foundation of the next town, Camargo, came as a direct result of Escandón's original colonizing scheme. The strategic location of this town was considered from a military and commercial point of view. A strong settlement thus located would necessarily check Indian invasions, and furthermore give impetus to the trade between Cerralvo and the Gulf coast settlements; and this in turn would encourage the opening of a highway into Mexico.[4]

On May 15, 1748, Santa Ana de Camargo was officially founded by Escandón with families from Nuevo León at a place where a settlement had previously been made. Don Blas María de la Garza Falcón, pioneer, ranchman, and Indian fighter, was put in command of both the military and civil establishments. One year after its foundation, Camargo became the base for the settlement of another town, Mier. Many well-to-do families from Nuevo León and Coahuila had been attracted to the first settlement and advantage was taken of this fact to use the surplus families in the foundation of Mier, in 1749.

Since the principal occupation of these people was either stock or sheep ranching they needed more pasture lands, and very early in the history of this section they began to cross the river into what is now Texas. In this they were encouraged by the authorities who saw in this movement the means of occupying the country north of the Río Grande.[5] Don Blas María de la Garza Falcón, founder of Camargo drove part of his stock across the river. His son Don Francisco de la Garza Martínez, whose land included sections 80 and 81 located north of the river, established himself at Carnestolendas[6] ranch at the present site of Fort Ringgold, Río Grande City, and by 1761, he had advanced to within five leagues of the mouth of the Nueces River, where another ranch, the Petronila, was located. Settlers from Mier and Revilla had also brought part of their cattle across into Texas as early as 1757.[7]

As has already been seen, Escandón was anxious for the establishment of settlements in the Nueces River region, and when in 1755 Don Tomas Sánchez asked for a grant of land on the north bank of the Río Grande; he was directed not to the land of his choice, but was told to seek for pastures in the land drained by the northern stream. Failing to find a suitable location, or not wishing to do so, Sánchez retraced his steps to the Río Grande and at Laredo established the second permanent Spanish-Mexican settlement on the north bank of the lower Río Grande.

When these settlements were created, no division of land was made but a common grant sufficiently large was set aside for the use of the whole colony. On account of the unsettled conditions of the country Escandón deemed it wise to wait at least fifteen years after the foundation of each town before making any private grants. Accordingly the first *visita real* donated the first grants in 1764. The notable thing about these settlements was that they were not made at the expense of the royal treasury but at the cost of either the captain, as was the case in Revilla, or at the expense of the settlers themselves.[8]

These settlements, which were in their infancy when the Mexican War of Independence came on, took little or no part in the liberating movement that swept the country. This inactivity was the result of the natural development and social and political condition of the settlements. In the first place the isolation and lack of communication with the rest of Mexico made actual participation in the movement impossible; secondly, all the energies and efforts of the settlers were directed to one objective; namely, protecting the frontiers from Indian attacks and depredations; and thirdly, the occupations and character of the people themselves did not tend to create or to foster political development.

Because of the lack of sufficient military protection, the Indians of this region were never wholly conquered. It is true that in some instances the colonists themselves were armed at the expense of the crown,[9] but because of the distance between the different settlements no united efforts were made to subdue the common enemy.

Spain, in spite of the wealth of her colonies, was going through a financial crisis at this time. As a measure of economy, the number of provincial officials was reduced. The viceroy, Marquis de Croix, was in favor of passing a law doing away with the captains defending the frontier. His idea was to substitute for these and their forces military detachments, whose duty would be the destruction of the savages [sic] then hiding in the mountains.[10] This proposal was bitterly opposed by Escandón, who knew too well the dangers to which the settlers were to be exposed. For a period of twenty-eight years, between 1764 and 1792, Indian hostilities ceased, but in 1792 the settlements at Mier, Revilla, and Laredo were again the victim of Indian attack.

Indian depredations did not cease with the independence of Mexico. The Indians had no compunction in attacking the settlements under the tottering but well-organized vice-regal government. The chaotic condition which existed during and immediately following the revolutionary period [here González is referring to Mexico's struggle for Independence from Spain (1810–21)] did not by any means inspire respect, much less fear, for the newly constituted republic. Conditions did not improve. As a protective measure against this evil and as a last resort Don Lucas Fernández, then governor of Tamaulipas, issued a proclamation in 1827 urging the frontier towns to arm and pay companies of soldiers to fight the Indians.[11] Apparently this did not improve the situation, for by 1835 the people at Mier, Revilla, and Laredo, had reached such a low degree of unproductiveness and their energies were so wasted by Indian warfare that they were unable to pay the contributions required of them.[12] So desperate was the situation that two years later, in 1837, *presidarios* or convicts were armed to check the invasion of the *bárbaros*.[13] This condition was also prevalent in the country on the north bank of the river, for as has already been stated the settlers of the Mexican border towns began as early as 1761 to establish their ranches along the right banks of the Río Grande.[14]

When two people of different races, customs, and traditions come in contact with each other disagreements, misunderstandings, and quarrels are bound to occur, even though their relations may be friendly to begin with. Place these two side by side after a war in which one considers itself the victim and views the other as aggressor, and the natural result will not be peace. This is what happened on the Texas-Mexican frontier after the independence of Texas.

Mexicans considered the Americans in Texas as interlopers no less than vandals, who had by deception and intrigue deprived them of one of their states. They looked indiscriminately upon all Americans as aggressors, waiting for the opportunity to deprive them of their personal possessions as they had deprived the mother country of a whole province. On the other hand, the Americans looked upon the Mexicans as a conquered, inferior race, despised because of their inability to check American advances. Because they were the conquered race the Mexicans were considered cowards and everything that was low and despicable.

Everything a Mexican did was wrong. During a period of lawlessness when both Mexican and American ranchmen stole freely from each other, the former paid the greater price. Whether Mexicans or Texans originated this illegal exchange of cattle is unknown, but the fact remains that it existed and that its existence led to many abuses and much bloodshed. While the big ranchmen prospered and profited, the small Texas-Mexican landowner was forced to abandon his property and either become a *peon* [a landless laborer] or leave the country. This state of affairs, which prevailed all over the border was no doubt created by racial and political enmity as well as by the avarice and cupidity of a few who wanted to get rich at the expense of others. As a natural result frictions were constant along the border. Due to the effervescent Latin temperament of the Mexican people, and to the fact that they considered themselves the offended party and the Americans the offenders, they as a rule took the initiative in the reprisal and revengeful moves.

Border troubles which occurred from 1840 to 1860 may be classified under two headings; namely, those motivated by personal resentment and enmity, and those having political objects as a base. Of those growing out of personal causes the famous Cortina raids are an example. The Wars of the Federation and the Carbajal revolution were political in origin. The fact that movements originated in Texas and received aid from its inhabitants, leads to the conclusion that the Texans knew of and favored them. Whether they participated in these movements through purely unselfish motives or through a feeling of enmity toward the Mexican nation is immaterial at present, but they took a very prominent part in the invasions of the Mexican border towns.

Just before the outbreak of the Texas Revolution Santa Anna, who had acquired power in Mexico as a liberal, came to the realization that the most suitable form of government for the country was a centralized republic. The disaster at San Jacinto on April 21, 1836 [The Mexican Army commanded by General Santa Anna was defeated at San Jacinto by Texan troops under the command of Sam Houston, effectively ending the Texas Revolution] checked his plans for a while, but once again in control, he proceeded to put them into execution. The liberal party was not of the same opinion as Santa Anna and showed its displeasure in true Mexican fashion—by a counter revolution.

This movement, which spread to the northern Mexican states, is of importance to Texas not only because it originated in the state but also because of the participation of a number of Americans in it. Hoping to give the northern states a better form of government, General Don Antonio Canales, a native of Nuevo León, led a revolt against the dictatorship of Santa Anna in 1839. His plan was to segregate the northern Mexican states and organize a new republic with a liberal form of government. Accordingly the republic of the Río Grande was proclaimed in Texas territory by Canales with much pomp and solemnity on January 18, 1840 [It is important to remember that between 1836, when Texas gained its independence from Mexico and the start of the U.S.-Mexico War in 1846, the territory between the Nueces River and the Rio Grande was in dispute, claimed by both Mexico and Texas. As González suggests here, the secessionist movement led by Antonio Canales (1839–40) complicated matters by claiming independence for the region].[15]

Many Texans who saw in this movement a way of retaliation and of furthering the disintegration of a nation already weakened by internal strife and the secession of a rebellious colony eagerly joined Canales. The creation of and the independence of this new republic was going beyond the expectations of the Texans. If Canales's revolt triumphed, the next step would be the annexation of the republic of the Río Grande to Texas. Canales who did not see this fact at first encouraged the Texans to enter his ranks. As an incentive, he offered volunteers a salary of twenty-five dollars per month, equal share in spoils, and a league of land.[16] Of the 600 volunteers who joined him, 180 were Texans.

Canales first came to the realization of the real motives of the Texans from a letter which H. W. Haines, commander of the Texas forces, wrote him. After asking for 150 head of cattle, Haines informed the Mexican general of his decision to march to Laredo and from there to proceed to the mouth of the Río Grande, probably Matamoros, at which place he would plant the Texas flag on the Mexican side.[17] Canales's belligerent attitude and reply proves that he had not suspected the Texans of any mercenary motives. He told Haines that any move on the part of the Texans towards Mexican territory would be considered an invasion and that if he persisted in the enterprise, he, Canales, would seek the aid of the federal troops to drive him out.[18]

Seeing that the war was endangering the sovereignty of the country, General Canales surrendered to the Federals on November 2, 1840.

Although no actual fighting took place on Texas soil, except at Laredo, the Texas border towns suffered materially as a result of the attacks [by the Mexican Federal Army] on Monterrey, Camargo, and Cerralvo, on which the settlers depended for their provisions.

No sooner had the *Centralista* trouble subsided than the border found itself in the throes of another uprising, the Carbajal rebellion of 1851.

Carbajal, who came from an old Spanish-Mexican family, was a Texan, and had been educated in Lexington, Kentucky and Virginia.[19] There, no doubt, he came in touch with American ideas of freedom and liberty (and there, no doubt, also learned from the same sources of the abuses and evils of the Mexican government). Like General Canales, Carbajal's plan was to offer armed resistance to the government at Mexico City; but he also had an immediate end in view as well; namely, to free the northern Mexican states of the Federal army, and to open up free trade between Mexico and the United States. The oppressive measures of the army had antagonized the inhabitants to the point of rebellion, while trade restrictions had brought them to the point of commercial and material starvation. A great number of Mexicans and Texas-Mexicans rallied at his head-quarters at Río Grande City. But he made a grave error; he allowed and encouraged the enlistment of Americans among whom were several Texas Rangers. The participation of Mexicans in a revolution was a legitimate if not patriotic pastime, but the invasion of Mexico by Americans was a thing that united all Mexican forces against the common enemy. Viewing matters in this wise Carbajal's men, although victorious in the first encounter with Federal troops, deserted their leader. Carbajal was then forced to flee and seek refuge in Hidalgo County. The remnants of his forces, Mexican as well as American, took advantage of the period of disorder to rob, sack, and plunder the border towns.[20]

But the worst and most far reaching in result of all Mexican border troubles were the Cortina raids. The descendant of a rich Spanish-Mexican family, Cortina was the "most striking, the most powerful, the most insolent, the most daring, as well as the most elusive bandit . . . that ever wet his horse in the muddy waters of the Río Bravo."[21] During his reign of bloodshed Cortina was the self-appointed champion of the Mexican border ranchmen, who saw in him the leader that would free them from American domination and rule. Although born in Mexico, he was a naturalized American citizen and as such held political control over the Mexican vote in Brownsville.[22]

On July 13, 1859 while in Brownsville, Cortina got into trouble with an American official who had arrested one of his servants. Justifiably or not, in his efforts to free the arrested man, Cortina shot and wounded the sheriff. Cortina then fled to Matamoros where he was hailed as the deliverer of the Mexican race in Texas. Some fifty men joined him; and from there he gave definite orders to kill Americans, to destroy their property, and to help the needy Mexicans.[23] This Robin Hood of the Mexican border became naturally the idol of a certain element among the border Mexicans. On September 28, 1859, the city of Brownsville found itself in the hands of Cortina and his men. His possession of the city was short-lived. With the aid of the Mexican forces at Matamoros Cortina was defeated and forced to retreat to his mother's ranch, the San José. While there he continued his role of liberator and issued proclamations to the Mexican people. In them he explained the purpose of his enterprise. This was, he said, to punish the infamous villainy of the Americans who had banded together to rob and persecute Mexicans, for no other reason than they were Mexicans by birth, and to organize a society of Mexicans in Texas whose chief efforts would be the extermination of the tyrants, and the improvement of the unfortunate Mexicans who resided in Texas.[24] With such impressive and high sounding words, it is no wonder that Cortina gained a large following. What his men thought of him may be gleaned from Major Heintzelman's report: "Cortina was now a great man. He had defeated the *gringos* and his position was impregnable. He had the Mexican flag flying in his camp and numbers were flocking to his standards. He was the champion of his race—the man who would right the wrongs of the Mexicans and drive the hated Americans to the Nueces." [Samuel Peter Heintzelman, a veteran of the U.S.-Mexico War was assigned to Fort Duncan just north of Eagle Pass, Texas, when the troubles with Cortina began (Thomas W. Cutrer, "Samuel Heintzelman," *Handbook of Texas Online*)].[25]

In March 1860 the following report was sent from Brownsville,

The whole country from Brownsville to Rio Grande City, one hundred and twenty miles, and back to the Arroyo Colorado, has been laid waste. There is not an American or any property belonging to an American, that could be destroyed in this large tract of country. Their horses and cattle were driven across into Mexico, and there sold a cow, with a calf by her side, for a dollar . . .

Rio Grande City is almost depopulated, and there is but one Mexican family in Edinburg. On the road this side I met but two ranchos occupied, and those by Mexicans. The actual loss in property can give but a faint idea of the amount of the damage . . . Business, as far up as Laredo (Laredo), two hundred and forty mile, has been interrupted or suspended for five months . . . There have been fifteen Americans and eighty friendly Mexicans killed. Cortina has lost one hundred and fifty-one killed; of the wounded I have no account.[26]

On December 23, Cortina with a force of approximately 500 men attacked the barracks at Fort Ringgold, Río Grande City, where he was defeated. He was driven out towards Roma, and later crossed the river at Zapata. Cortina continued his guerrilla warfare, making flying attacks, plundering and pillaging the Texas border towns.

During the Civil War period, which was contemporary with the French invasion in Mexico [1863], Cortina ceased his activities in Texas and became a general in the patriot army that was fighting the invaders. The triumph of the Republican army in Mexico accomplished, Cortina renewed his attacks on Texas soil. Conditions along the border became intolerable. The United States government then asked the Mexican authorities to cooperate with the border officials in the capture of the chieftain. Accordingly in 1873 Cortina was made the personal prisoner of Don Porfirio Díaz, then president of Mexico.

The arrest of Cortina brought to a close international raids and attacks by organized bands of men. The close of this period of warfare and bloodshed left the two races with an antagonistic feeling of hatred and distrust toward each other that was not ameliorated by the abuses that in the name of justice were committed by the Texas Rangers against the Mexican population prior to and during the revolution in Mexico. [The increasingly violent conflict between Anglos and Mexicans in South Texas eventually culminated in a native-born insurrection that took place between 1915 and 1917. The *Mexicano*-organized irredentist movement, popularly known as the *Plan de San Diego,* called for the unification of Mexicans, Indians, Blacks, and Japanese under a "Liberating Army for Races and People," whose purpose was to throw off the yoke of "Yankee Tyranny" and reclaim the borderlands for a multicultural nation. During this time, quasi-military groups of "from twenty-five to a hundred men" raided Anglo ranches and farms, derailed trains carrying goods to and from the Valley, burned bridges, and sabotaged irrigation pumping plants. The *Plan de San Diego* was ruthlessly and brutally squashed through the combined efforts of Texas Rangers, informal deputized posses acting with the support of Anglo ranching and mercantile enterprises, and the threat of American military intervention. At the height of the insurrection, the military threatened to bombard and occupy the town of Matamoros, believed by many to be the center of Mexican organizing, and the entry point of outside agitators and revolutionaries. After the "border troubles" came to a halt in 1917, it became clear that the insurrection had profoundly negative effects on the very population whose interests it sought to protect; between five hundred and five thousand Mexicans were killed as a result of retaliatory violence following the insurrection, while only sixty-two Anglo civilians, and sixty-four soldiers lost their lives during the struggle. The armed conflict of 1915–17 represented the culmination of the decades long struggle between the old *Mexicano* ranching culture and the new agrarian economy in South Texas. In *Anglos and Mexicans in the Making of Texas*, David Montejano notes "most of the guerrilla activity took place in the four counties where commercial agriculture had made the greatest inroads—Starr, Hidalgo, Cameron, and Willacy." Interestingly, two of these counties were the focus of González's master's thesis (Montejano 116–25).]

CHAPTER 2

History of the Settlements at Zapata, Roma, Río Grande City and Brownsville

Racially and historically all Mexicans whether in the mother country or out of it, belong to three distinct groups: *criollos*, *mestizos* or half breeds, and Indians. The *agraciados* or holders of land belonged to the first group. The colonists for Camargo who had been recruited in Nuevo León were in the majority Spaniards of good character and well-to-do. Among them were to be found men of prominence such as Don Nicolás de los Santos Coy, ex-alcalde of Cerralvo. With the exception of twelve *mestizo* heads of families the rest were Spaniards. Referring to Camargo, Escandón said that this settlement was destined to become a big city, not because of the advantages offered by the land but because of the desirable character of the citizenship.[1]

Speaking of the settlers of Mier, Don José Tienda de Cuervo refers to them in the *Inspección de Nuevo Santander* as being "small in number but of good quality and well-to-do."[2]

It was, then, the people from these frontier towns, Guerrero,

Camargo, and Mier, and not undesirables, who began migrating across the river into Texas after 1757. The ranches they established formed the nucleus of the frontier towns which were later to develop. In Zapata County are to be found two unimportant but interesting towns, San Ignacio and Zapata. San Ignacio was founded in 1830[3] by Don Jesus Treviño, a native of Guerrero, on land which was part of the old Vasquez Borrego grant. He bought this land from the descendants of the grantee. Zapata was settled by people from Guerrero, who, having ranches on the Texas side of the river, came to make their homes there.

If the happiness of a country depends upon its having no history Zapata County should then by rights hold first place in this; for nothing of interest or importance has ever been recorded of its history. A county thoroughly Mexican and rural, it has been untouched by progress and development. The people continue living their placid existence becoming only aroused when Americans try to buy or lease their land. During the wars of the Federation in 1840 General Canales crossed with his army into Guerrero, but no actual fighting took place. A fortress which was constructed in 1851 for protection against the Comanches still stands in the main street of San Ignacio. The loop holes on its sides tell of struggles these settlers must have had with the savages [sic].

Although Zapata County was untouched by the Civil War, it played its part during the cattle thieving raids which were so common during that period. A history of the region says:

On April 11, 1863, a party of cattle thieves passed over into Mexico near what is now called Zapata, driving quite a herd of stolen Texas cattle. Captain Santos Benavides of the Confederate Army followed them into the very town of Guerrero, Mexico. Although he did not capture the thieves, he drove them out of the country. Captain Benavides took with him but 30 men and was ordered by the Mexicans to retire from Mexican soil, it being alleged that he was violating the treaty between Mexico and the United States, but he refused to do so until he should communicate with the Mexican alcalde [mayor] and obtain assurance of a cessation of the banditti operations on the Texas side.[4]

The same sentiment which has kept these people from selling their land to Americans came into view on June 15, 1915, when a number of Zapata people joined the Carrancista troops in retaliation for the punitive Pershing expedition sent into Mexico.

Starr County, organized in 1848, joins Zapata on the south. The two leading towns there are Roma and Río Grande City.

Roma, a Mexican town in its entirety, was founded as a result of a grant, by a royal *cédula* [document] in 1767 to Don Juan Salinas and Don Juan Angel Saenz. A few years after the grant was made sons of Saenz crossed the river with their families and established the beginning of a settlement at Los Saenz and at Rancho de Buena Vista. By 1848 the development of Buena Vista raised it to the dignity of a villa and its name was changed to Roma. Although history does not mention Roma in the Mier expedition it was only a few miles from there that Cameron and his men marched into the Mexican town of Mier. Before the Civil War the establishment of a fort at Roma was contemplated by the United States government and Negro troops were sent there for the purpose. The land-owners were very much opposed to these troops, however, and refused to sell or lease to the government. During the Civil War, Roma was the center from which cotton was sent to Mexico. This produce was taken in carts by way of Matamoros and thence to Tampico from whence it was sent to Europe. During the border trouble originated by the revolutions, which started in Mexico in 1910, Roma served as an outpost and canton-ments were built, but no permanent garrison was ever established there [Roma, Texas was also Gonzalez's birthplace].[5]

The first settlement at Río Grande City was made probably in 1757 by Don Francisco de la Garza Martínez, a son of Don Blas Maria de la Garza Falcón. The Martínez lands included sections 80 and 81 located north of the river.[6]

Because of the many Indian invasions which desolated the whole countryside the ranch established on the Texas side was not perma-nently inhabited; the owner made periodical and occasional visits whenever conditions permitted him. After an attack in which Don Francisco was killed and his two daughters were taken prisoner by the Indians, the family did not return to Texas but left the property in the hands of the servants.

The Garzas, the original owners of the land have many descendants living in Starr County. Many of the Garzas married Texas people. One of the Garza girls married Henry Clay Davis a Kentuckian who came with Taylor's army of occupation. After his marriage in Camargo, Davis came to Texas, and on property inherited by his wife built the first cabin which was to be the nucleus for the present city of Río Grande. Rancho Davis, as this settlement was called, soon became a thriving town. Three steamboats which came from Brownsville made this settlement the trading center for the nearby ranchers.

Davis who was a far seeing and practical man wanted at all costs to organize the territory in which he lived into a county. Although the community did not have the number of inhabitants required by law, Davis succeeded in his attempt by bringing people from Camargo.[7]

During the fifties the Americans and foreigners who came were all single men. But they did not remain so for long; they married the daughters of the leading Spanish-Mexican families and made of Río Grande City a cosmopolitan little town.

Such names as Lacaze, Laborde, Lafargue, Decker, Marx, Block, Monroe, Nix, Stuard, and Ellert, among families who claim the Spanish language as their own, show the mixture of races in the native element of the town [here Gonzalez forecasts historian David Montejano's claim that mid-nineteenth century Anglo settlement in Texas was accomplished through a "structure of peace" that often involved strategic marriages with powerful grant-holding Mexican families].

Fort Ringgold, the military center for the lower Río Grande country, is located at Río Grande City. It is one of the first garrisons established in Texas after the state was admitted to the union. This fort forms part of a chain of garrisons built in accordance with a system of defense adopted on the western frontier. It was named in memory of Major David Ringgold, Fourth Field Artillery, who was killed at the beginning of the Mexican war at the battle of Resaca de la Palma, near Brownsville.[8] The first lease for this fortress was drawn up in 1859.[9]

At that time the nearest railroad was at Laredo, one hundred and ten miles distant, but that was no disadvantage, for the Río Grande was navigable and three steamboats plied its waters.

During the Civil War, when Brownsville was taken by the Union forces under General Banks, a few of the Federal troops came to Fort Ringgold. Except during the Cortina raids (1859–62), there have never been any further attacks on the fort.

At the outbreak of the Spanish-American War in 1898 all troops were removed from the fort, although state militia was sent to occupy it during the period. In 1900 a company of Negroes was stationed there. Immediately trouble arose between the colored troops and the Mexicans, who resented their permanency in the town. Conditions grew tense, the Mexican population took the offensive, and as a result the Negro troops raided the town. [González is referring here to the 9th Regiment of the U.S. Cavalry, also known as the "Buffalo Soldiers," who were assigned to Fort Ringgold upon their return from the Cuban front of the Spanish-American War (where they fought heroically alongside Teddy Roosevelt's Rough Riders in the charge up San Juan Hill). On November 20, 1899, second lieutenant. E. H. Rubottom ordered that a Gatling gun be fired on the area between the Fort and the town in response to what he believed was an attack on the Fort by the townspeople of Río Grande City. Though no one was seriously injured, the incident brought greater scrutiny on 2nd Lt. Rubottom and the troops under his command. Eventually, the governor of Texas, Joseph Sayers, ordered that the 9th cavalry be replaced by white troops ("Fort Ringgold" *Handbook of Texas Online*).]

During the Díaz regime in Mexico conditions were peaceful along the border, nothing extraordinary occurred, and it was thought wise to remove all troops from Ringgold and move them to San Antonio. The fort property was turned over to the Department of the Interior, and in 1912, the land was surveyed, divided into town sites and put on the market. But the Madero revolution in Mexico changed all plans. Because of the isolated location and the nearness to a Mexican town Fort Ringgold was the place where difficulties might have arisen during the trouble with Mexico following the death of Madero, but nothing of consequence ever happened during this critical period.[10]

Matamoros, founded in 1765, under the name of San Juan de Esteros, became Matamoros in 1821. Nuevo Santander, which extended northward as far as the Nueces River, became Tamaulipas after Mexico's independence. Since this state controlled its public lands, it allotted to prominent Mexican citizens and soldiers all vacant lands then found between the Río Grande and the Nueces River.[11]

The annexation of Texas to the United States in 1845 brought to a close amicable relations between Mexico and the United States. In February 1846, the United States, anticipating war sent General Zachary Taylor to Corpus Christi from whence he continued his march to Brownsville. It was while he was there that Fort Brown was constructed under his supervision. On May 7 and May 9 of that same year the battles of Palo Alto and Resaca de la Palma were fought respectively just a few miles from Brownsville. Negotiations for peace came to an end with the Treaty of Guadalupe Hidalgo on February 2, 1848. Immediately after the treaty was ratified Americans began to come to the Texas border, and with their arrival trouble came.

The outbreak of the Civil War saw a line of United States garrisons at Fort Brown, Fort Ringgold, and Fort McIntosh. The Confederates controlled the Valley territory until 1863 under the command of General Bee [Confederate brigadier general and former Texas legislator (1849–59)]. A number of Mexicans who served under this officer revolted at Ramireño, killing a Mexican and former sheriff. This act caused Bee to suspect the loyalty of all Mexicans and some of the Texans as well.[12]

Hearing of General Bank's [Major General Nathanial P. Banks, a Union commander stationed at New Orleans] plan to capture Brownsville, the Confederates set fire to the garrison and to several bales of cotton and retreated to the King Ranch at Santa Gertrudis. To make matters worse, 8,000 pounds of powder stored at the garrison caught fire. The city was in such turmoil that the organization of a home guard was deemed necessary to assure order in the city. With the aid of Americans and several Mexicans from Matamoros, General José María Cobos, a Mexican refugee then in Brownsville, carried this plan into effect. Cobos, who was an imperialist, crossed into Matamoros with the men he had rallied under his command at Brownsville and declared his intentions of aiding the cause of Maximilian [Maximilian I Austrian-born emperor of Mexico from 1864–67]. His plan proved unsuccessful and he met death at the hands of Cortina.[13]

A historian of this region says that in 1864:

Matters on the Río Grande as far as the territory east of Laredo is concerned, remained quiet until early in June when Captain John S. Ford, having recuperated his forces up to 1,200, began systematic guerrilla warfare on all outposts. He was very successful in these operations, so much so that, on June 16, he occupied Río Grande City, the Federals withdrawing toward Brownsville.[14]

From June 23, 1864, to April 9, 1865, the date on which the last battle of the war was fought, a series of skirmishes occurred in and around Brownsville. The following table shows the place and result of each:

June 26, 1864 — Captain Ford advances from Río Grande to Edinburg.
June 25 — Captain Ford attacks the Federals at Las Rucias, Federals defeated.
July 30 — Captain Ford enters Brownsville.
August 9 — Confederates attack 81st Negro Engineers. Confederates retreated.
September 6 — Colonel Day attacks Boca Chica. Defeated.
September 26 — Mexia, Imperialist general, enters Matamoros; Confederates join him.
October 14 — Confederates take Boca Chica.
October 1864 – January, 1865 — guerrilla warfare between Liberals and Imperialists in Matamoros.
May 9, 1865 — Last battle of the war.[15]

The year 1910 saw the end of Mexico's rule of iron and the beginning of anarchy and chaos in the republic south of the Río Grande. As might be expected Brownsville, of all border towns, because of its strategic position, both from a commercial and military point of view, and the fact that it was made the target for rebel attacks from Matamoros, became the military center for the frontier. The first of these disturbances occurred in February 20, 1913, when the officers in command at Matamoros threatened American citizens there unless a loan was secured from them. This loan, which was made in the form of a command, not as a favor, caused the county judge and the sheriff of Cameron County to communicate with Governor [Oscar B.] Colquitt. State troops were rushed to Brownsville and for a while it seemed as though intervention might be unavoidable.

In April, 1913, General Lucio Blanco, a follower of Carranza entered Tamaulipas, and on June 3, attacked the city of Matamoros. Seeing that the United States government objected to his method of "forced loans and ransoms," he directed his exactions against all foreigners.[16] A period of looting and vandalism followed which, however hard the United States tried to stop it, could not be checked. Matamoros remained in the hands of Carrancistas until March, 1915. Bandit attacks were prevalent and very common during the border troubles of 1915–16. It has been estimated that:

> One hundred Mexicans have been executed by the Texas Rangers and Deputy Sheriffs without process of law. Some place the figure at 300. Most of these executions, it has been asserted, were by reason of data furnished the Rangers implicating the particular Mexicans in the raids which were occurring.[17]

The period from 1865 to 1910 is characterized on the border as an age of bandit raids and cattle thief raids. This era forms one of the most romantic and picturesque epochs of the frontier.

> Mexican and American outlaws have always found an asylum along the Río Grande border, where they might escape to either side according to necessity. Their living has depended chiefly on illegal foraging and marauding. Due to the depredations of these disreputable men, stock raising along the lower border, and even as far north as Corpus Christi, was dealt a severe blow during the period from 1867 to 1876.[18]

Bandit attacks were common and the border people, both American and Mexican found themselves in a constant state of agitation and preparedness. The stage lines and the mail were robbed and travelers were never safe. As a check to all these disturbances the Rangers were sent in 1875, with Captain J. F. McNelly at their head.

While stationed at Río Grande, McNelly was notified that a band of cattle thieves was operating at Las Norias, a ranch two miles from Sam Fordyce. The Rangers pursued these men across the river into Mexico, captured the Mexican town of San Miguel de las Cuevas, and drove the cattle back to Texas. A similar encounter occurred at Edinburgh a year later, in 1876.[19]

The two incidents mentioned above are merely examples of what was common occurrence on the Texas border. Conditions improved by 1900, for:

> Upon the advent of the railroad and the beginning of canal work for the many irrigation schemes along the Río Grande, the population of the Valley rapidly increased, the newcomers being principally speculators from northern states with their complement of land-seeking tourists who wished to live in a milder climate and a large number of laborers from Tamaulipas, Mexico, and other points further in.
>
> Proportionate to the number of new settlers, comparatively few murders or killings took place, although thieving became a profession so that almost every family in the Valley suffered the loss of their fine blooded stock.
>
> During the thirty years immediately preceding 1915, although many persons had been caught and tried for cattle-thieving, few had been convicted. Political influence had been a prime factor in the trial of many malefactors, and it is alleged that by reason of the inability of a good jury to convict a really guilty man the inhabitants became indifferent.[20]

In comparison with earlier times, peace has come to the border. And although there are as many Mexicans in these counties as there have ever been, perhaps more, conditions are changed. The wealthy Texas-Mexican of the towns is by slow degrees becoming a part of the American population; the country gentleman, although still conservative and a Mexican at heart, now begins to see that his material welfare depends upon his becoming an American citizen. Among the poor, the gun is forgotten and the plow is substituted. Realizing that peace is conducive to prosperity and happiness, they are willing to lay aside their feuds and their enmity toward Americans and become a part of the state.

CHAPTER 3

Present Mexican Population in the Counties Considered

W hatever original grants exist in the border counties are classified either as Viceregal or Mexican grants. The former are those which were parceled out by the Visita Real in the last half of the eighteenth century to the colonists of Nuevo Santander. The latter, the Mexican grants, issued between 1830 and 1835, were given to leading Mexican citizens of the northern Mexican states. This was done to encourage the movement of Mexican colonists into Texas with the hope that it might serve to counter balance the influx of American colonization in the province.

The viceregal grants in Texas were merely an extension of the original grants given to the colonists at Camargo, Mier, and Guerrero, and extended to the north side of the Río Grande. The Mexican grants are located in what are now Kleberg, Brooks, Duval, and Jim Wells counties. In Kleberg County, the land included in all these grants is now part of the King estate. Don Domingo Rotge, descendant on his mother's side from the holder of the Boveda grant of 1831, is the only Texas-Mexican who now owns any property in this section of the country [here González refers to the infamous King Ranch which spans some 825,000 acres across four counties in South Texas. Ranchers Richard King and Gideon Lewis began accumulating land in 1853, by purchasing (and sometimes pilfering) lands originally granted to Spanish and Mexican settlers].[1]

Approximately 60 percent of the big landowners in the counties under consideration, Zapata, Starr, and Cameron are descendants of the original grantees.[2] The acreage owned by the landowners dating back to the original division of land is not very large, due to family division of property. However, with this as the center, large estates have been created such as the Yzaguirre and Guerra holdings in Starr County and the Cuellar and Vela properties in Zapata County. [It seems that González's decision to focus her study on Cameron, Starr, and Zapata counties was based on the patterns of landownership in South Texas. Her research clearly centers on counties in South Texas in which Mexicans retained some measure of control over land and resources.]

Another class of landowners is that which comprises Mexicans who came after 1848 and have purchased property on the border. The recent revolutionary troubles in Mexico which began in 1910 have added to this number of property owners. The Canales and González families in Jim Wells County, the Perez and García families in Duval County, and the Ramirez and a branch of the Guerra family in Starr County are examples of this group.

Since 1900 another class of property owners has arisen. The small farmer, whose property may range from a few acres to a few hundreds of acres. This class has been created by the converging of the two classes which prevailed for many years in the border: the landed proprietors and the working masses. In cases where the landlords have been forced to sell, the cowboys, renters, and servants have purchased small parcels from the former owners, thus elevating themselves to the landowner class.

The development of the Río Grande Valley, the growth of towns, the interest in education, and a desire for more comforts has taken great numbers of the country day laborers or *jornaleros* to towns and cities. The exodus of these people into the towns has brought still another class of landowners into existence, the owners of town lots. This class consists of two groups: the temporary and the permanent town lot owners. In towns such as Río Grande City, Roma, Zapata, and even Brownsville, the town-lot owners are different from those living in the counties not bordering on the river. These are frontier people, *mestizos* of the border middle class who, ambitious for their children, have come to town to send them to school. As a rule these people are farmers or small ranchmen in moderate circumstances. The house they construct in town, usually a temporary home, is a small frame building of the box house type. Ordinarily it consists of three rooms only. In spring when school closes these houses are abandoned until the following fall when the children return to school.

The other group permanently establish themselves in the towns, where they usually get work. They become clerks in stores, truck drivers, and not seldom laborers. Their principal ambition is to be property owners, and with the first savings they buy a lot. Like the other group of town-lot owners they build inexpensive, small frame houses.

The following tables show the percentage of Mexican property owners in the border counties. The numbers speak for themselves and show to what extent the Mexican element predominates.

DUVAL COUNTY

Population	9,000
Total property owners	1,594
Mexican property owners	1,336
Percentage of Mexican owners	83.73
Non-Mexican property owners	258
Percentage of non-Mexican landowners	16.27

ZAPATA COUNTY

Population	4,500
Total property owners	470
Mexican property owners	464
Percentage of Mexican landowners	99.38
Non-Mexican property owners	6
Percentage of non-Mexican landowners	0.62

Population	4,200
Total property owners	3,993
Mexican property owners	3,314
Percentage of Mexican landowners	83
Non-Mexican property owners	679
Percentage of non-Mexican landowners	17

JIM HOGG COUNTY

Population	4,500
Total property owners	544
Mexican property owners	397
Percentage of Mexican landowners	72.9
Non-Mexican property owners	147
Percentage of non-Mexican landowners	27.9

The roll books in Cameron County were not accessible when the writer was there; however, the County Clerk gave this percentage as approximately correct: 60 percent of the population is Texas-Mexican and 64 percent of the property owners belong to the same race.[3]

CHAPTER 4

Social and Economic Life before the Development of the Lower Río Grande Valley

Transportation in the border counties was backward and un-developed. The scarcity of railroads made communication al-most impossible. There were two methods of transportation in this region; by land and by water. The former was carried on by ox-cart caravans that combed the country. The latter by steamboats which plied the Río Grande and formed the faster and safer of the two. The earliest date concerning navigation on the Río Grande is April 28, 1828. On that date the Mexican congress gave a concession to John Davis Bradburn and Stephen Staples to introduce steamboats in the Río Grande. When trouble with Mexico started in 1846 and transportation was most needed, Major John Saunders, engineer in the United States Army, employed an experienced seaman, Mifflin Kennedy, to help him in selecting boats that would be suitable to ply the Río Grande waters. Four boats were purchased and these did valu-able service in transporting General Zachary Taylor and his troops to

Fort Ringgold at Río Grande City. All boats on the river were used as freighters between Brownsville and the mouth of the river, and those sufficiently light came as far up as Río Grande City.[1]

Previous to, during, and after the Civil War, Brownsville was the trade center for the lower Río Grande Valley. This town was not only the nucleus from which exports and imports were sent to and from Mexico, but an extensive commerce was carried on with New Orleans. Merchandise from the Louisiana towns and from others in the upper Mississippi were brought to supply the needs of this region. It is estimated that during 1880, one hundred and twenty-five steam and sailboats entered Brownsville. Local merchants sent from one to two[2] hundred thousand dollars to New Orleans every two weeks and one boat alone in one trip carried 1,400,000 dollars in merchandise.[3]

During the period of the Confederacy the people of the lower Río Grande looked to Mexico for trade and upon the Río Grande as the means of transportation rather than to the region between the Nueces and the Río Grande.[4]

In 1872 the water at the mouth of the Río Grande became so shallow that it was impossible for ships to enter the harbor. All freight came in through Brazos de Santiago, where the boats were unloaded and the merchandise was taken in trains of wagons to Point Isabel and Brownsville. The trade which came in through this port satisfied the needs of the people and the lower Río Grande Valley became "a little independent republic." That same year the Río Grande Railroad was built, and was used for transportation of goods from Brownsville to Point Isabel. Merchants soon became dissatisfied with the excessive rate that they had to pay and in competition with this railroad citizens from Brownsville and Matamoros re-established the "Fast Freight" wagon transportation.

For a period of twenty-two years from 1882 to 1904 little or nothing was heard of the lower Río Grande Valley country in the United States. This may be due to two factors. First, the yellow fever epidemic in 1882 which devastated the country; and second, the construction of a railroad from Corpus Christi to Monterrey which connected with the Mexican National Railroad extending into southern Mexico. This railroad killed all the trade which had heretofore gone to the states of Chihuahua, Durango, and Zacatecas by way of Brazos de Santiago. It was not until 1904, when the St. Louis, Brownsville, and Mexico railroad was completed that Brownsville became again a railroad center.[5]

Prior to 1900 the only means of transportation in the rural communities was by means of ox-carts. Regular ox-cart caravans carried ranch produce to the towns. Laredo was the trade center for the territory north of Río Grande City and for Zapata County; Brownsville for the country bordering Starr County in the south. Whether these trains were owned by one individual, or whether several cart owners went together for protection, these slow moving trains were hired by ranchmen when necessity arose. Twice a year these ox-carts plied their way to Laredo or Brownsville loaded with wool, horsehair, hides, and bones. In turn they brought back the necessities of every day life—groceries, dry goods, candles, *piloncillos* [Mexican brown sugar pressed into a cone shape]. Corpus Christi was another trade center, but not as safe as the first two named. For, on the way to either Laredo or Brownsville these caravans met only friendly Mexicans, while on their way to the coast they were in danger of meeting armed Americans who sometimes for no reason except that the drivers were Mexican killed those who fell in their hands. A well-known Texas writer refers to this period in the following terms:

> During the fifties and sixties Mexicans were doing a great deal of freighting in Texas. They were hauling in their ox-carts, from the coast to San Antonio and from San Antonio to Chihuahua and other points in Mexico, goods to the value of millions of dollars annually. In 1857 the intense feeling against Mexicans took the disgraceful form known as the Cart War. This Cart War was nothing less than an effort on the part of certain Texas ruffians to run Mexican freighters out of business.[6]

The isolation which resulted from the poor means of transportation and retarded the political development of the border communities has also tended to create a patriarchal life and foster a spirit of conservatism among the people there. Eighteenth-century customs, traditions, and beliefs brought by the first colonists still prevailed at the beginning of the nineteenth century in many of these communities. Rural life was pastoral in its simplicity, the necessities of life were few and the government a paternal hierarchy.

In his fortress-like home, built more for protection than for comfort, the landowner lived like a feudal lord; he was master not only of the land which he possessed but of the *peóns* who worked the soil.

The landlord had certain duties toward his servants and they in turn had specific obligations to perform. He was the protector in time of danger, the adviser and counselor, and not seldom the judge who tried the case as well as inflicted the punishment. Besides these moral duties the master had material obligations toward his *peóns* and their families. He furnished their living quarters, and besides the payment of a small sum of money, six *reales*[7] a day, provided them with some articles of food. The salary, "*cuatro reales y la comida o seis reales y comen de ellos*," "four bits and meals, or six *reales* and furnish your own" was in effect until fifteen years ago.

The servant class was composed of two distinct and separate groups: the cowboy and the *peón* proper. The former, either *mestizo* or *criollo* was a fiery-spirited man, wild if you please, over whom the master had no control. He disliked law and restraint, hated innovations and newcomers. The open range was his haven and as he galloped across the prairie horse and rider appeared as one. The *vaquero*, or cowboy, was the product of the frontier, son of the small landowner who did not have enough to occupy him at his own ranch.

The *peón* on the other hand was of Indian blood, immigrant from Mexico whom the landowner had brought to Texas to work. He was submissive to his master's orders, obeyed blindly and had no will of his own. He never rose to the dignity of being a cowboy, but was either a goatherd, worked the fields or performed all the menial labor around the ranch. This class also furnished the personal servants of the ranchman.

A closer relation existed between the *peón* and master than between the *vaquero* and the ranchman. To the former the *amo* or master literally meant being master, to the latter the landlord was merely the owner of the cattle he punched. A social, racial, and economic gulf separated the *peón* from the landowner; on the other hand the *vaquero* might rise to the level of his more fortunate associate.

Since the *peón* received very small remuneration for his work he was always in debt to the ranchman. In case of necessity, of sickness, or death the master furnished the money, and this formed a debt which the *peón* could never hope to pay. Besides debts similar to these, the *peón* was cursed with the debt which was inherited from his father. This was the food debt which accumulated year after year and made the *peón* a serf to the land. It came into existence from the fact that the landlord discouraged *peóns* from trading or buying in town. To prevent this he had general stores at the ranch where the *peón* might buy all he needed, from patent medicines to calico. All goods were sold on credit and at a very high price. An unfortunate situation resulted from this system, it gave the master absolute power over the *peón*, and this control converted him into a machine whom the landlord could work at his will. The *peón* realizing his position grew pessimistic and developed a spirit of hopelessness and despair. There was no incentive for him to save, since whatever he might save by economizing went to the landlord. The master exercised complete control over the *peón*, economically and socially as well as in religious matters. He might be the possessor of a goat, a few chickens, and a pig, and these only if he kept them within his own enclosure. Neither did he cultivate any soil for himself. In the backyard of his *jacal* his wife might plant a few rows of corn, of beans, and a few pumpkin vines. On the other hand, he was allowed the use of as many milk cows as he needed, and when the master butchered, he was allotted a certain amount of meat.

Socially, the *peón* was as subservient to his master as he was economically. The fact that the *peón* was economically dependent caused all the evils resulting from this system of peonage. Let us suppose that the *peón* wanted to take his family to a dance at the next ranch, or perhaps to town. Since he had no means of transportation, he depended upon the master for the use of a wagon, a team of horses, or an ox-cart. This method, which depended entirely upon the personal attitude of the master, his prejudices, likes, or dislikes, was too uncertain for the happiness of the *peón* and his family. The same thing happened in time of sickness, no physician could be summoned without the master's advice. This does not necessarily imply that the landlord was cruel or unjust. This custom was merely part of a system that had been inherited by both classes. Neither one nor the other knew of a better plan, the unfairness and injustice of it was never realized by the master, and the *peón* looked upon it as a thing that had to be. If a son was to be married the master was consulted and his consent was assured by accepting to ask for the girl's hand. If a girl was asked in marriage, the father did not recognize the formal engagement until the master gave his sanction.

The *peón's* living quarters were in keeping with his material position. It consisted of a one-room, thatch-roof, dirt-floor *jacal*, which served as a living room and bedroom as well. The kitchen was a still more miserable hovel, often roofless, and many times without a fireplace. A portal or arbor made from dry corn stalks, which served as a dining room during the summer months joined the kitchen to the house. An earthen pot *olla* covered with canvas, the water cooler of the ranches, was suspended from a beam of the portal and the gourd dipper hung from a hook attached to another. The furniture was the most rudimentary type. Most of it homemade. Often the bed consisted of four poles dug into the dirt floor with boards across it, no springs, and a grass mattress. A few chairs, a table, and a small mirror, hung on the white washed wall, completed the furniture of the *peón's* home. But in every home, however humble it might have been, a statue or an image of Our Lady of Guadalupe, enshrined in paper or natural flowers, occupied the place of honor.

Many of the amusements among the working classes, with the exception of dancing, perhaps, are of a religious nature, such as the feast of St. John, of St. James, and the day of the Holy Innocents.

Dancing was the most important and interesting form of amusement. At times the dances were held in the open. The dirt floor was smoothed and sprinkled and packed with boards until it was as hard as a brick. Rough lumber benches were arranged in a square around the dance floor; a kerosene lantern furnished the only light. Everyone, young or old, from the toothless old grandmother who smoked her shuck cigarette to the toddling baby, attended. Early in the evening the guests began to arrive in all their glory. The orchestra which occupied a prominent place and ordinarily consisted of a guitar, a violin, and an accordion was kept busy all night. The dance began early. The mothers, rigid and silent, were the dragons who watched over their daughter's behavior. No decent, well-bred girl ever talked to her partner while dancing, and if she danced two sets in succession with the same partner she gave rise to scandal. By midnight the dancers were enveloped in a cloud of dust which from a distance appeared like a whirlwind and the dancers like spirits of the desert. At sunrise after playing *La Golondrina,* the orchestra and the dancers went home, not to sleep but to engage in their respective duties. For two or three weeks after the dance the rural mail was loaded with proposals of marriage. The popularity of these country belles depended upon the number of love letters they received after the dance.

On some ranches St. John's Day was also celebrated by a dance, and in those nearest the river by what was known as *correr el gallo.* This picturesque but brutal custom, now extinct, was a test of the ability of the horsemen participating. The man owning the fleetest horse was the *corredor* or runner. In his hands he held a rooster to whose feet and wings had been tied gaily colored ribbons, as many as there were contestants. The runner stood some twenty feet from the other riders. At a given signal all started running, the goal of each horseman being to see who could get the first ribbon. Needless to say little or nothing remained of the original rooster by the end of the contest.

Early on Saint John's Day everyone got up at dawn and went to the nearest stream to bathe. This was done in commemoration of Christ's baptism by John in the river Jordan. This innocent custom has given rise to the belief among certain people that the Mexican working man bathes only once a year. It was the belief among girls who still prided themselves upon having long hair that if part of their hair was cut off on this day it would be four times as long by the next anniversary. So on a mesquite block, and chopped off by an ax, the young ladies sacrificed their hair in honor of Saint John.

The 28th of December, the day dedicated to the memory of the Holy Innocents, was a time of much fun and merriment. People played pranks and jokes on each other. It was Halloween and April

Fool's Day combined. It was the one time when the Mexican child could with impunity misbehave to his heart's content without fear of parental punishment.

New Year's was a day of thanksgiving. Watch parties and dances were common. An amusing, practical, and romantic game was matching boys' and girls' names; practical, because the young man had to give his partner an expensive present, romantic because this was the beginning of a courtship.

All Mexican national holidays were celebrated by the people with dances, speeches, and *vivas* to Mexico.

Some twenty years back when sheep were plentiful, the time of sheering was an occasion for much merriment among the workers. Shearers were hired from all the surrounding country for the season, which lasted from a few days to two weeks according to the number of workers and sheep. There were always some among them who played the guitar or the accordion. Needless to say, singing, dancing, and love making were never lacking. Or after the evening meal it was customary to sit under the old *portal*, sing *tragedias* or love songs, and tell stories of ghosts, apparitions, and treasures. Some of the stories told were so weird and frightful that in hearing them some were afraid to go home in the dark.[8]

Far different from the wretched existence of the *peón* was that of the landed proprietor. His was a life of easy-going simplicity, not without its charms. Proud, aristocratic, and a gentleman by inheritance, he retained those characteristics in the wilderness in which he lived. He prided himself upon two things: that he was a Mexican and the land he possessed had been his for generations past. The first characteristic was deep rooted and the one endeavor of every ranchman was to make his ranch a miniature Mexico. The family was encouraged and expected to keep intact the customs and traditions of the mother country; the servant class was commanded to follow in the footsteps of their brethren in Mexico.

In his large, strongly built stone or adobe house, the *ranchero* led a patriarchal existence. As head of the family his word was authority, no other law was needed and there was no necessity for civil interference. An offense, whether criminal or moral, met with severe punishment.

Paternal discipline was harsh and strict. The old border proprietor showed no compassion when justice demanded a severe punishment. A father disinherited two of his children because they were gamblers[9] and another horsewhipped his son with rawhide leather thongs because he had stolen a calf.[10]

A man was expected to have his escapades, in fact the more conquests, the more of a Don Juan he was, the greater the glory to his name. But woe to the woman, wife, daughter, or sister, who dared by her actions to besmirch family honor. An action which in a man was overlooked as insignificant was an unpardonable offense for a woman. As the depository of family honor, woman was always under the direct rule of man. When she married she passed from her father's dominion to that of her husband's. As in most Spanish countries, her position was a contradiction. She had complete control in the home management, yet she lived a life of conventual seclusion. Married at an early age, and not for love, but for family connections and considerations, she made a submissive wife and an excellent mother.[11]

These women lived, if not in luxury, at ease, and had all the comforts attainable in those days.

Characteristically Spanish, the rich landowner did not do any of the manual labor himself. He supervised the farm work and rode out to the pasture with the *vaqueros*. He was a characteristic figure as he rode away, a picture hardly conceivable in the United States some years past—he wore a broad brimmed Mexican felt sombrero, short jacket, and tight fitting trousers. During sheep shearing time when a thousand or more head of sheep were sheared, when the calves were marked and the cattle branded, he was there to direct the work.

The rich, in their pretentious stone houses, square and flat roofed in appearance, lived not unlike other frontier people, ever in readiness to receive friends or foes; the former with open arms and the latter with ready arms. A warm welcome awaited friends, a hot and exciting one enemies.

These homes, monotonous and uninteresting from the outside, were the center of border culture and refinement, not the refinement of the East or of Mexico, but of a culture which had originated and developed in a community which,

On the farthest border of our territory and without the means of rapid transit to and from the great centers of population, combined with (the fact that) half of its inhabitants were foreigners who clung to the traditions and customs of their native country . . . retarded the growth and nurtured procrastination in developing its natural advantages. The sociology of these people for nearly half a century past is peculiarly remarkable and borders upon the romantic, replete as it is with incidents of pastoral ease and plenty, urban success and luxury, intermarriages and social seclusion; moral courage and freedom from crime.[12]

The inside arrangement of the house was typically Spanish. The principal room of the house was a big *sala* or living room where the family sat and talked in the evening. Deer, wild cat, and coyote skins took the place of rugs; mounted deer heads, powder horns and hunting guns hung from the walls. Adjoining this *sala* was a smaller one where the ladies entertained their friends. Only the daughters had their rooms in the house proper. When the sons came to be a certain age their rooms were in the men's quarters in a nearby building. The kitchen and dining room formed a separate establishment.

The furniture in these homes was of the best that could be bought at Brownsville, Matamoros, or Laredo. It was very common in these border ranches to find beautiful carved beds with tall canopies and silk draperies, marble top dressers and tables. Family portraits, often hand-painted, pictures drawn by the young ladies of the family, samplers, and tapestries, hung from the walls.

Perhaps the most interesting room of all was the kitchen, with its enormous fireplace often occupying one end of the room. It was about three feet from the floor and enabled the cook to do the work standing. The iron and copper pots and skillets hung from nails on either side of the fireplace; and to prevent fires the kitchen had a dirt floor.

The oven, a mound-like structure was built outside. The process of heating it, although rudimentary, was very effective. Burning coals were placed inside and the door was closed air tight; when the inside walls were red hot, the coals were removed and the corn or flour cakes were baked in a very short time.

The dining room with its huge beams across the roof, big, home made table and benches was always ready to welcome the host of friends, travelers, and transients who visited the ranch. In those days any traveler who passed by the ranch during meal hours was invited to share the hospitality of the ranchman. A similar custom prevailed about giving lodging for the night at whatever ranch night overtook the traveler.

The amusements of the Texas-Mexican gentleman were the same as those of the rich in any Spanish or Mexican community. Races, the chase, gambling, cock fights, and dancing occupied most of their time. The holding of fairs in certain communities and at stated times was the occasion for horse races and cock fights in the daytime and gambling at night. The best racing horses from the border country both in Texas and in Mexico were brought to these fairs for the occasion. Large sums of money were staked and fortunes were made and lost both at the races and at the gambling table. Professional gamblers from Mexico journeyed to the fairs in search of easy money.

The dances that were given by the owners of the ranches marked the social feature of the year. To these functions were invited all the landed aristocracy from the surrounding country as well as from the towns. The ladies came in the family coach, escorted by mounted cavaliers who rode by the side of the carriage. The dances gave occasion to the ladies to display their finery and their charm.

An orchestra from town furnished the music, waltzes, polkas, and schottisches. A midnight dinner was served, wine was drunk, and toasts were offered the ladies, and a convivial atmosphere prevailed throughout the evening. This was the only form of amusement that women shared with men.

The families from the neighboring ranches visited each other, the men talked business, discussed their love affairs, and drank wine in the *sala*. The women on the other hand entertained their guests in their own parlor and no doubt enjoyed a topic that is dear to every woman's heart; gossip and clothes.

Life in the towns such as Brownsville and Río Grande City was gay, exciting, and even turbulent. The army camps stationed there, the nearness to the Mexican towns, and the coming of officials from across the river added a touch of romance and color to border life. [González delves more deeply into the "romance and color" of border life in the nineteenth century in her co-authored historical novel, *Caballero* written in 1938.]

Social functions, especially the dances that were given in Brownsville, were bizarre and cosmopolitan. Mexican officials, their gold epaulets gleaming in the candlelight, United States officers, the town *caballeros,* danced and mingled together. American women, and star-eyed, flashing dark beauties laughed and talked in the same language, Spanish. The flower of the Spanish-Mexican society, with the American and Foreign element—French, German, and Spanish—formed the select society of the border towns. The description that follows was written by one of the belles of Río Grande City:

Society was different in those days to what it is now. The men were more gentlemanly, the ladies more gentile [genteel]. The dances were held in what is now the old courthouse. The officers from Fort Ringgold and their wives were the honor guests. There were neither racial nor social distinctions between Americans and Mexicans; we were just one family. This was due to the fact that so many of us of that generation had a Mexican mother and an American or European father.

If a gentleman courted the favor of a young lady, he sent her a bouquet of flowers, which she, if she accepted his attention, wore on her breast that night. We wore muslin or organdy dresses in the summer, and in the winter silk or satin. We preferred walking to the dances in those days, and following the old Spanish custom, were not escorted by young men, but were accompanied by a chaperone. A reception committee which stood at the door escorted us to our seats. The young men went as stags and stood on one side of the hall, and it was only when the orchestra preluded the piece that our partners came to us. The set ended, we were again escorted to our seats and with a bow the gentleman thanked us for the honor of having danced with us.

All the men except the army officers, who were in uniform, wore formal clothes. And when refreshments were served do not for one moment think that we had a little punch like you have now. A banquet does not do justice to the dinners served at these dances. The gentlemen served us and saw to our needs. The end of the dance finished our good times, but not for the men, who serenaded the town until daylight.

The arrival of a steamboat was also occasion for much gaiety. Everyone went to the river to meet it to see the strangers that might come and receive the news from the United States.[13]

All Mexicans regardless of their racial descent or political affiliations are essentially Catholic. And this is true of all, whether in Mexico or Texas. There existed among the more educated border people a certain group of men who priding themselves upon their liberal tendencies, were unfavorable to the priests and opposed the Church. These men were the product of the Mexican school. As boys these men had been sent to study in the mother country and came back imbued with liberal ideas, Masonic tendencies, and looked upon the Church as a nest of conservatism. And yet, contrary to their convictions, they married Catholic wives and educated their daughters in Catholic schools. But according to their self-made creed religion was only for women and children.

These anti-clericals only went to church three times in their lifetime, and of the three they were taken there at least twice by a woman; when they were baptized, when they were married, and when they were taken by their family to receive the last rites for the dead. They, among themselves, might attack the Church because it was theirs to do or undo at their will, but woe to the Protestant who dared to slander it. Mexican Protestants were social outcasts, and there was nothing more contemptible than these in the eyes of the border Mexican.

Due to the lack of communication, the distance from the towns and the lack of priests, the country districts were often neglected. From time to time, as often as possible, the missionary priest made occasional visits to the ranches. He was a familiar figure, beloved by all, who brought happiness and consolation to these out of the way *rancherías*. These black-robed Oblates rode long distances on horseback, alone through a country infested with bandits, and often suffered actual want as they went from ranch to ranch. No account of the border will be complete without mentioning Father Joseph Marie Closs, the father of the border who for fifty years was priest, physician, and adviser in the most forgotten and forsaken districts of the region.[14]

Father José María, as he was called by his parishioners, was born in France on February 17, 1826. When a young priest, not more than twenty-eight or thirty years old, he was sent as a missionary priest to the lower Río Grande. For a period of fifty years he was the outstanding character in that section of the country, whose word was followed by all, from the political boss[15] to the rich town merchant and the working-man. His life was the life of the people among whom he lived. His parishioners who were to be found in a territory scattered in the wilderness of the border counties were his spiritual children in every sense of the word. He baptized, married, and buried them. He laughed with the happy, wept with the sad, comforted them in their vicissitudes, and ministered to them in their sickness. He was a picturesque figure as he rode through the border country on his white horse, wearing deerskin leggings, and a broad-brimmed hat tied under the chin. Because of his ability as a rider he was known as the "cowboy priest."

On a certain occasion, as he was going from Roma, the seat of his parish, to a ranch he lost his way and was without food for three days. When he arrived he was so weak that he spat blood. On being offered the only thing available at the ranch—meat—he would not eat it because it was Friday. "My food," he said, "is to do the will of Him who sent me." At the time of his death in 1907, he was still an excellent rider, he walked erect and with a steady step, and his mind was as clear as ever.[16]

Border magnificence and hospitality were displayed in full when the priest came to one of these ranches. All the people from the adjoining ranches came, the landowners with their families, the cowboys, and the servants. Preparations were made for the event days in advance, bread and cakes were baked, cocoa beans roasted and ground and made into chocolate squares; a cow or calf was butchered, hens were dressed, and the unused quilts and mattresses were aired. The servant's quarters were astir with excitement, the girls looked forward to getting a new sweetheart, the boys with anxiety to see new girls. The servant women were kept busy grinding corn on the *metate* for *tortillas,* others washing linen to be used for the altar.

Those homemade ranch altars were the joy and pride of feminine art. At one end of the *sala* a sheet was hung to the wall; and on it were constructed with varicolored ribbons, red, yellow, orange, and blue, arches and arcades that would have made an architect blush with envy. Sprays of cedar, oleander, and artificial flowers were pinned here and there making the already impossible arches more impossible still. Pictures of saints and angels formed a celestial host, and holy statues, some of wood and some of marble, were placed on the altar table.

At twilight, while the people were still arriving, the priest told his beads as he walked up and down the patio. After supper all came to the improvised altar to recite the Rosary and hear a sermon. After each decade of the Rosary the hoarse voice of the cowboys and servants mingled with the tenor of some ranch singer and the voices of the women and children in praises to the Mother of God.

O, María, Madre mía	O Mary, Our Mother
O, Consuelo del mortal	Consolation of all mortals
Amparadme y guiadme	Protect us and guide us
A la patria celestial.	To our celestial home.

It is only within the last twenty-five or thirty years that the Mexican border people have become interested in public school education. There was no need for it. The wealthy sent their children to the schools in Mexico, principally Monterrey and Saltillo, those in moderate circumstances sent theirs to private Mexican schools in Texas, while the children of the servant class did not attend school at all. In fact, the landowners discouraged the working classes getting an education on the ground that this would ruin them for the work they had to do.

Since the aim of the border people was to retain their racial characteristics and character intact, parents took the necessary steps to attain this end, and this was to give their children a Mexican education. The result of this retarded the assimilation of the Mexican element with the American population. Those who studied in Mexico came back with ideals that were far different from those of their American neighbors. They were altogether Mexican in spirit and sentiment, were proud of the fact, and made no effort to understand American principles. They came back with a concentrated hatred and distrust toward the United States, a country that in their opinion was the natural enemy of Mexicans.

The private schools which formed the bulwark of Mexican conservatism in the border counties were systematically organized and followed a course of study superior to that offered by the public schools in either Starr or Zapata County. The aim of this system of education was threefold: to maintain a Mexican spirit in the youth of the border by imparting Mexican ideas and ideals, to uphold these by a thorough knowledge of national traditions and history, and to arouse pride of race. As in Mexico separate schools for boys and girls were encouraged, and a course of study similar to that of that country, and which included Mexican history, civics, morals, and ethics, and manners, grammar, general science, mathematics, reading, and writing was employed.

Since the definite and ultimate aim was the formation of a well-mannered Mexican youth, the teaching of history, morals, ethics, and manners received especial attention. "Morals" was taught by the use of stories, fables, and by discussions on such subjects as *Tolerance, Heroism and Women, Modesty, Woman and the Home*.[17] Simplicity in dress and manner, dislike of worldly things and self-sacrifice, were inculcated in the minds of young girls. All girls were encouraged to imitate Sor Juana Inéz de la Cruz who in her humility had as a girl cut off her hair, saying, "Of what use is adornment on a head that is empty?"

Extracts from a little manuscript on manners and ethics will show what was expected of the border boys and girls:

Preceptos peculiares a los niños en sociedad con las señoras
Precepts peculiar to boys when in the company of ladies

A todas las señoras
tratar procuraremos
con la atención más fina
que es debida a su sexo,
el más comodo asiento,
el que nos sirvan ellas
jamás permitiremos
si estamos en la mesa
y cuando en algún juego
con ellas concurramos
a su gusto sujetos
con toda política
nos manifestaremos
sus faltas perdonando
llenando sus deseos
cuando sean decorosos
arreglados y honestos.

Ladies must be given
the utmost attention that
is due their sex. We must
give them the most comfortable
seat, and never allow
them to wait upon us at
the table. And when
we play a game with them
we must excuse their
mistakes and obey all their
desires provided these are
their place, decorous and
decent.

Lección 2a
El que es cortés y fino
procura con esmero,
cuando concurra un baile
el convidar primero
a bailar las señoras
que a malquistado el tiempo,
los hombres o tienen
cualquier otro defecto.

Lesson Two
When at a dance he who
is courteous and refined
should first invite the
ladies that have been ill-
treated by time, or who
have any other defect.

Preceptos peculiares a las niñas   Precepts peculiar to girls

---

Lección 4a
En las acciones todas,

Lesson Four
Be modest in all your

Manifestad modestia,
no cruces las rodillas
ni recarguéis con fuerza
la espalda en el asiento;
procurad que descienda
el vestido hasta abajo
cubriendo el pie, y se advierta
desencia en vuestros ojos,
pues es cosa muy fea
el mirar con descaro
y es cosa aún mas perversa
procurar de los hombres
las miradas, pues esta
de una mujer perdida
es la señal mas cierta.

actions, never crossing
your limbs or leaning heavily
on the back of your chair.
See that the dress
descends to the floor,
covering your feet and let
modesty be reflected in
your eyes. It is improper
to look daringly at any
one and it is very
perverse to try to catch
the eye of men.
This is the certain sign
of an immoral woman.

Lección 5a
De la compañia de hombre
el huir, aunque no deban
las mujeres, es malo
anhelar por ella,
con otras de su sexo
debían de estar contentas.

Lesson Five
Although women should
not flee from men's company
it is a bad thing to
always wish for it. They
should be content with
the company of their own sex.

Lección 6a
Hablarás con reposo
con juicio y con reserva
para que los que os oigan
no imaginen ni crean
que pretendéis mostraros
instruídas; que esta
idea ofendiendo el orgullo
desprecio os acarrea.[18]

Lesson Six
Talk with repose and good
judgment so that those who
hear you may not think that
you pretend to appear a
blue stocking. This besides
being offensive will
bring you the disdain of all.

These schools operated from six to ten months a year depending upon the financial conditions of the community. The finances were in charge of a Board of Directors whose duty it was to assure the teachers their salaries. In many cases the wealthy people of the community contributed a certain amount of money for the maintenance of the school. When the Board did not have the means to meet all the expenses the parents were then assessed so much per month.

An oral, annual public examination was held at the close of the scholastic year. A Board of Examiners known as the *réplicas* composed of the leading Mexican citizens decided whether the children passed or failed the year's work. During the examination, which lasted from two to five days, the children were examined in all the subjects studied. On the evening of the last day an entertainment was presented in honor of the patrons. The hall was decorated with Mexican flags, laurel wreaths, and pictures of Mexico's heroes hung from the wall. The evening's program, which consisted of plays, patriotic recitations, and songs, was closed by the most solemn and impressive number—the singing of the national hymn. Fourteen girls dressed in white, wearing the red, white, and green draped across their breast, sang the national anthem. It was then that the men who came there to shed patriotic tears took out their handkerchiefs with pride. Mothers whispered to their little ones the meaning of it, and told them of a country that had once been theirs, but had been snatched away by American greed.

A school of this type, El Colegio Altamirano, founded in 1897 with an enrollment of over one hundred children, is still in existence. The following extract which appeared in a Mexican newspaper gives an account of one of these examinations:

> The annual examinations which closed the scholastic year of El Colegio Altamirano, of which Miss Angela Ramirez, modest and intelligent teacher, is the principal, began May 27. For more than three decades this school maintained by the Mexican colony of Jim Hogg County has imparted the knowledge indispensable to the future happiness of the student. The Mexican colony at Hebbronville is making superhuman efforts to maintain a school, not only for its own welfare but primarily to honor the land which was given to us by the noble, liberty loving Mexican insurgents.

The principal, Miss Ramirez, began by examining the lower grades. The children answered in a satisfactory and efficient manner, leaving the Board of Examiners as well as the spectators very much impressed by the improvement. In the afternoon the examination was continued at the appointed hour.

The following day the high school children were examined. These students proved very competent in all their studies. We were very much gratified to view the exhibition of manual labor, writing, drawing, and painting.

It might be said with pride that the work presented by *El Colegio Altamirano* shows the noble efforts of the Board of Directors, and the patrons who are making great efforts to improve the intellectual conditions of their children, and who are also endeavoring to uplift the name of their country in a foreign land.[19]

The first private school of any sort in this region was the Convent of the Incarnate Word opened in 1853. Seeing the need of teachers and religious instructors on the border, Bishop Audin, the first Catholic bishop in Texas, prevailed upon the Incarnate Word Sisters in France to come to Texas. In 1852, with the Pope's consent, four Sisters sailed from Havre, and one year later opened the doors of the convent that has received and educated the daughters of the conservative Texas-Mexicans of the border.

Besides the elements of ordinary and secondary education religion, music, painting, plain sewing, fine needlework, and embroidery were taught. In 1893 the tuition per month for day pupils was from fifty cents to three pesos and for boarders, fifteen pesos Mexican currency. The school year consisted of two terms of five months each. In 1857 this institution received a charter from the State Department of Education allowing it the privilege of graduating its pupils.[20]

St. Joseph's school for boys saw its beginning in 1865 as a small parochial school. The great number of Mexican children in attendance necessitated the bringing of Mexican teachers to this school. This institution, which consisted of three departments, primary, intermediate, and high school, had a varied curriculum. The fees were reasonable and within the limits of the average parent. Another school for boys, between the ages of five and thirteen, opened in 1887 under the direction of the Incarnate Word nuns. A Presbyterian free mission school for Mexicans was established in 1878. This school, which consisted of primary and intermediate departments, was conducted entirely in Spanish and Spanish textbooks were employed. English was taught as a foreign language.

The public school system of Cameron County, organized in 1875, permitted the creation of independent school districts if so desired by the majority of the voters. For fifteen years after the organization of the public school system classes were held in some of the old Mexican buildings. But in 1880 the construction of a school building was begun.

Speaking of the type of children attending the public schools a writer expressed himself in these terms:

> Nearly two-thirds of the population of Brownsville are Mexicans, and the same proportion applies to the scholars attending the public schools. The majority of them could neither speak nor understand the English language when admitted to the schools, and from the fact that they seldom hear anything but Spanish spoken at home, it will be readily seen that infinite patience, and versatile talents were called for in the teachers who undertook the task of Americanizing these young sprigs and buds of our sister Republic.[21]

Public school education was far more advanced in Cameron County than in either Starr or Zapata counties. The fact that Brownsville was a commercial and army center, and that it had communication with the rest of the country caused it to progress more rapidly than the other communities mentioned. Up to 1910 public school education in Starr and Zapata counties could not have been worse. The teachers were the product of their respective communities who could neither speak nor write the English language. What little instruction they received in English was acquired from teachers in the same circumstances who held county second grade certificates. When a group of boys and girls belonging to the privileged class, that is the landowners, reached the age, not the education, required of public school teachers they applied for a second grade certificate. The questions with the answers were handed out by the examiner, who in exchange for this favor received a certain percentage of the teachers' salary. The distribution of teaching certificates among the elect became a political issue and a means of controlling votes. The tax-payers who assured the political boss the greatest number of votes was sure of getting certificates for all his sons and daughters.[22]

The rural school buildings were *jacales*, thatch roofed huts with dirt floors. There were neither blackboards nor desks of any kind, the pupils wrote on slates and sat on crude backless benches or on boxes. What little teaching was done had to be conducted in Spanish. The alphabet and numbers were learned in English, and "America" was sung in a pronunciation that would not have been recognized by any English speaking person. These rural schools lasted from six to seven months, and the salary received by the teachers ranged between forty and fifty dollars a month, a fortune in those days when Mexican currency was used altogether.

At Río Grande City, the county seat conditions were better. There had arisen a group of young teachers, who although they had received no normal school training could at least speak the English language. These were the descendants of Americans who married Mexican wives.[23]

Unfortunately the early public school records have been destroyed, and no statistics can be obtained earlier than those of 1914. But from these we may gather what conditions were some twenty years back. The following data were gathered from the scholastic report of 1914–15:

CAMERON COUNTY

Number of teachers	69
Number of teachers holding first grade county certificate	0
Number of teachers holding second grade county certificate	32
Number of teachers holding second grade state certificate	18

Number of teachers holding first grade state certificate   0
Number of teachers holding permanent certificate   8

STARR COUNTY

Number of teachers	42
Number of teachers holding first grade county certificate	1
Number of teachers holding second grade county certificate	37
Number of teachers holding first grade state certificate	1
Number of teachers holding second grade state certificate	4

ZAPATA COUNTY

Number of teachers	24
Number of teachers holding second grade county certificate	0
Number of teachers holding first grade county certificate	24^{24}

Parents did not send their children to the rural public schools for two reasons; firstly, the teachers did not know anything to teach and secondly Mexican schools offered better opportunities to the pupils. The teachers in these private schools were graduates either of the Saltillo or Monterrey schools and had a superior education to the native instructors.

Such was life in the border before the development of the Río Grande Valley brought hundreds of middle class Americans from all sections of the United States. Heretofore, the American families who had come previous to or after 1848 had become Mexicanized, adapting themselves to the existing conditions in the border. The onrush of the new Americans, eager to make a fortune, anxious to accumulate wealth as soon as possible, changed the placid, easy-going life that had existed in the border counties. What these changes are and what the outcome of these has been will be discussed later. The Texas-Mexicans, as American citizens are now going through an important period of transition that will no doubt decide their social and political status for the future.

CHAPTER 5

Border Politics

The treaty of Guadalupe Hidalgo in 1848 determined definitely that Texas was no longer part of Mexico's territory, but that it formed part of the United States of America. Soon after this treaty the region was divided into a number of counties, Nueces, Cameron, and Starr.

The movement of Americans to this region was slow, while the Mexican population increased by leaps and bounds both by immigration from Mexico and by the natural increase of a prolific race. In 1850 the population in these counties was 8,500, in 1880, it had increased to 50,000, while by 1910, the population had doubled that of 1880.[1]

The type of Americans who came were over ambitious men who soon bought out the small Mexican landowners, and became the cattle barons of the border. Like the big Texas-Mexican landowners, they became the lords and protectors of the men who worked for them. The fact that the Mexicans were Mexicans in their own eyes and were unwilling to assimilate, made their masters consider them foreigners.

When these Texas-Mexicans automatically became American subjects, according to the terms of the treaty of Guadalupe Hidalgo, they found themselves unprepared for American democracy. Mexican politics, to which they were accustomed, were politics of the sword and revolution; manhood suffrage was almost unknown to them and certainly never practiced. The vote which had been given to them as by a miracle meant nothing to these newly created American citizens.

It was then that bossism originated. It grew as a necessity at first. The need of instructing these new voters was evident, and if to the victors belong the spoils, the votes of these men belonged to those who were intelligent enough to herd the voters together. Here were hundreds of voters who were willing to do as they were bid. The political bosses who arose in those early days cannot be said to have been unscrupulous politicians, they were in reality a Godsend to the organization of political life.

The first boss of the lower Río Grande region, "the genius of the democrats," was Colonel Stephen Powers, a native of Maine. The Mexican war found him a lawyer in New York City. He enlisted in the army and came to Texas. As a colonel, he commanded the American garrison at Matamoros. After the war was over he remained in Brownsville, where he became a power both with the Americans and the Mexicans. If in his treatment of the Mexicans he was often harsh and severe, he acted according to frontier ethics. However, he cannot be said to have been unjust, and he cannot be accused of being unfair.[2]

Powers was farsighted enough to see that the perpetuation of the power of the Democratic Party depended upon his successor. In 1878, just four years before his death, he made Jim Wells his partner. Wells was reared in Matamoros and Brownsville and understood the psychology of the border Mexican. The fact that he was a Catholic gained him the confidence of the Texas-Mexican element. His power, which lasted from 1880 to 1920, consolidated the power of the Democratic Party and made an impregnable and powerful *bloc* out of the Mexican vote. Speaking of the Texas-Mexican people Wells expressed himself in these terms:

> The Mexican people, if you understand them are the most humble people you ever knew . . . They are largely like the Indians in that respect. Their friendship is individual. For instance you have a great many friends among them, and they would

follow your name and your fortunes; and that is the way it is . . .
I suppose the King Ranch people control over 500,000 votes
and they, the Mexicans go to Mr. Caesar Kleberg, and to Rob-
ert Kleberg, and to Captain King — while he was living — and
ask them who they should vote for. The truth is, and very few
people who don't live in that country know, that it is the property owners and the intelligent people, who in that way do really
vote Mexicans, and that is the truth about it, and any one who
has lived there can see the worth of it, if they know it.[3]

As far as the Mexican population was concerned, Wells belonged to
the category of political bosses. When asked whether he considered
himself one he replied:

So far as I being boss, if I exercise any influence among these
people because in the forty-one years I have lived among them,
I have tried to so conduct myself as to show them (the Mexicans) that I was their friend and they could trust me. I take no
advantage of them in their ignorance, I buried many a one of
them with my money, and I married many a one of them; it
wasn't two or three days before the election, but through the
years around, and they have always been true to me and if it
earned me the title of boss, every effort and all my money went
for the benefit of the Democratic ticket, from president to con-
stable, and if that is what earned it, I am proud of it.[4]

The tremendous increase of population, the introduction of irrigation, and the increase of transportation facilities coincided with the
decline of Wells. His fall was due to the fact that conditions were
getting too diversified for one man, and primarily to the coming of
Americans. Because of Mexican clannishness, and a reverence for the
past, the political condition of the counties where the Mexican element predominates still remain, very much as it was in the time of
Well's ascendancy.

In some of the border counties, especially Cameron and Starr,
politics has been in the hands of a small class of landowners. These

hold tenaciously to family traditions and possess a Mexican culture perfected to the nth degree. They hold latifundian estates and because of the power derived from this fact, hold political sway over the Mexican vote of their communities. And when this vote is controlled, the result of the local campaigns is assured. Although true to their Spanish traditions, the men in these families have always been conscious of their American citizenship, and have exercised their rights.

Perhaps the most characteristic of these border families is the Guerra family. They hold dynastic sway over Starr County, their word is law and like feudal barons they do and undo at their will. The founder of the family was Don José Alejandro Guerra, who as surveyor of the Crown came to Mier in 1767 and received *Porciones* 80 and 81.[5] Part of the Grant extended into Texas, and two temporary ranches were established by the Guerras in Texas, Las Escobas and El Blanco. However, the head of the Guerra clan in Starr County was not born in Texas but at the family home in Mier, in 1856. He attended El Colegio Civil in Monterrey, and at the age of fourteen came to Corpus Christi to learn the English language. In spite of the wealth of his family, he preferred to learn English by working rather than by attending school. He clerked at the George F. Evans Mercantile Store, and thus learned the language in a practical way. In 1876 he returned to Mier, where he served in the *Guardia Civil.* The next year he came to Roma where he engaged in the mercantile business. There he married Miss Virginia Cox, the daughter of a Kentuckian and a Mexican mother.

As a businessman, a banker, a ranchman, and a politician, Guerra has been surpassed by no other Mexican in the border. Early in his career he realized that the Mexican element in his country needed a leader, and since he had political ambitions he became an American citizen. In a short time he was the recognized leader of the Democratic Party, and the right hand man of Wells.[6]

His financial success, his magnetic personality and handsome appearance made Don Manuel Guerra a leader of his people. He became a political boss because the people were willing to follow him and wanted him to be one. He accomplished his political control by three methods, first through family relations, second, through financial aid, third, by giving the elect political positions. All the land-owners in Starr County were a branch of his family or were related through marriage; he afforded credit to the ranchmen at his stores and issued teacher's certificates to his favorites in exchange for votes.

The Republican Party was organized in this county not for political convictions but for personal enmity and hatred. All Don Manuel's enemies, regardless of their political creed became Republicans. The political campaigns and elections of the Reds and Blues, as the Democrats and the Republicans became known, were bloody and rivaled the Kansas election of 1855 in corruption. The following quotation is a brief history of the leading campaigns in Starr County.

Among several political campaigns, in the county affairs, there were three that attracted the public attention in a very remarkable manner. The first one took place in 1888 when the local parties put up their tickets, one headed by W. W. Shely, candidate for sheriff by the Reds, or Democrats: the other ticket headed by Don Lino Hinojosa, well known Republican. In this election, it is said that Don Lino had two to one, but the election was contested and due to the fact that Hinojosa did not know the English language he could not take possession of the office. The result was this: Shely kept the office as a Democrat when he was really elected by the Republicans.

The next turbulent campaign took place in 1900 when Mr. Ed C. Laseter, the wealthiest man of Falfurrias, took the lead of the Republicans and selected Domingo Garza as candidate for sheriff. Again W. W. Shely was the head of the Democrats in 1900.

This was a bitter campaign, as the candidates made speeches casting undue reflections on their respective opponents in offices. The limit was reached when Domingo Garza, Republican candidate, was placed in jail under the charge of conspiracy to murder the sheriff. This happened on Sunday and it was said that this was planned in order that he could not have any magistrate to fix his bail. By next Monday evening R. B. Rentfro, a prominent lawyer from Brownsville, was here to attend the case and joined by J. P. Kelsey, they had Garza out on bond. The election kept going on; the case was transferred to Hidalgo County District Court and tried during the first term, where the charge was found to have no merits and the case was dismissed. This hurt the Republicans very badly, as they were beaten in the election, although it was a well-known fact that the Democrats had to call on outside help, as was proved by many red flags left on the Río Grande River stuck in the sand bars in several crossings as in Azunas, Las Ajuntas, and Barreras. This act of extreme free suffrage gave the natural results and the leader of the Republicans, Mr. Laseter, appealed to the state legislature to have a new county made out of the northern end of Starr County. A bill was introduced by Mr. Brooks, but as it is required for a certain number of square miles to form a county, it was necessary to run into another county and the bill was opposed, but Mr. Laseter [sic] never gave up and after failure in two or three legislatures, the bill finally passed. Brooks County was created and Starr County was deprived of its best soils for grazing, pasturing, and farming purposes.

The last campaign, probably the most bitter of all, as it had the odor and color of human blood, took place in 1906, when W. W. Shely, on account of sickness, resigned from office, and Deodoro Guerra was appointed sheriff by the County Commissioners' Court. Naturally, being the sheriff and supported by the Democratic leadership, he became a powerful man. Close to them was, Gregorio Duffy, who had been chief deputy sheriff under Shely and county tax collector, but who was disappointed that he did not receive the appointment, and got out of the Democratic ring. Then he, with a number of sympathizers, made a swing towards the Republicans and supposing to make a stronger ticket, he was nominated sheriff by the Republicans.

This campaign was always sadly remembered, as both parties established a weekly issue (wrongly called newspapers), the Republican under the title of "*El Picudo*," which had two meanings, one "Boll Weevil," the other "Streamly Chatter," this was edited in Río Grande. The Democrats published at El Colorado

Ranch under the title of "*El Verde de Paris*" (Paris Green), which is the name of a poison to combat the boll weevil, but did not stop the chattering. Neither paper resulted in anything but irritating the political spirit of the voters on each side.

Meanwhile the parties kept having their regular meetings at their respective headquarters. The Democrats rounded up their sympathizers in the lot of the old Court House, at present where the primary children of Río Grande City attend school. The Republicans gathered their men in the large lot of Don Lino Hinojosa.[7]

Both Republicans and Democrats imported votes from across the river. Don Manuel issued a call for help to all his kinsmen and supporters, who sent their workers and their respective henchmen. The night previous to the election both the Democrats and the Republicans caroused all night, the former enclosed within the walls of the Court House, the latter in a corral belonging to Don Lino Hinojosa, Republican leader, This was done to prevent the antagonistic parties from stealing voters from each other.

On the night of November 1, Sheley, Democratic candidate was murdered in bed by an unknown hand [*sic*; it was the district judge, a Democrat, who was murdered in his sleep the night before the 1906 election ("Guerra, Manuel," *Handbook of Texas Online*)]; and while the Democrats mourned the death of their candidate, Duffy, the Republican leader, took control of the election. The Democrats were driven out of the Court House and were not allowed to vote. Riot ran high, there was shooting and drinking in the streets of Río Grande City, and the people did not dare go out. The Democrats called on the Rangers for help and in the meantime the city was placed under martial law.

La Grulla, a small town near the county seat was strongly Democrat, and the Republicans determined not to permit the arrival of the ballot box. A party of armed men proceeded toward La Grulla with this in mind. On the way they had an encounter with the approaching Rangers whom they mistook for the La Grulla people. Under the surveillance of the Rangers the election, which turned out to be a victory for the Democrats, took place. This was the last of the bloody election. [Not quite, in January of 1907, Gregorio Duffy was killed in a gunfight by Deodoro Guerra, the newly-elected sherriff. Though Deodoro Guerra and his cousin, Democrat powerbroker Don Manuel Guerra were indicted for conspiring to murder a federal official (Duffy was a U.S. Customs officer at the time of the gunfight) both were eventually acquitted ("Guerra, Manuel," *Handbook of Texas Online*).]

Don Manuel Guerra continued in power until 1915, the year of his death. Politically the Guerras still control Starr County in spite of the opposition presented by the American population of the region. The present generation of Guerras have one advantage over Don Manuel, they all have been educated in American colleges and universities. As lawyers, bankers, merchants, and politicians they continue the work of their fathers.

The social and economic condition of the border people before the development of the Río Grande Valley and the coming of the Americans to the border was discussed in chapter IV. These two factors revolutionized border conditions, socially, economically, and politically as well.

When the newly arrived Americans came, people in moderate circumstances who came with the idea of increasing their fortunes, they found a political situation that shocked their sensibilities as good American citizens. Unaccustomed to politics as prevalent in the border, they condemned the Mexican-Americans as ignorant people who were unfit to have a vote. In coming to this rash conclusion these people did not realize that politically the Mexican-Americans have not been given a square deal and that they have never known anything but corrupt politics.

Whether fit or unfit for citizenship, the fact remains that these people form part of our social structure, and must be treated accordingly.

Public schools in the border have not been conducive to the mental development of the individual, much less to the political improvement of the region. The fact that the greatest percentage of the population is rural, and does not speak the English language explains the backwardness of the inhabitants.

But since 1900 when economic and industrial conditions caused the exodus of Mexicans from the ranches to the cities the situation has altered. The children of these small landowners and ex-laborers in town have attended American public schools.

> They have profited from the superior educational and economic advantages thus afforded as well as from contacts with the new settlers who have poured in from all parts of the South and Middle West . . . there has arisen in their midst a class of prosperous, educated citizenry whose living conditions and attitudes compare favorably with American standards.[8]

It must be remembered, however, that in old Texas-Mexican towns such as Laredo, San Diego, Río Grande City, and Brownsville there has always existed a group of educated, cultured Mexican families who have always been leaders in their communities. From this class and from the newly created urban middle class have arisen men who, conscious of the needs of their less fortunate fellow citizens, want to bring them out of the political apathy to which they have succumbed. These new leaders are anxious to awake the Mexican-American to the realization that they are American citizens and that as such they must demand and exercise their rights. In order to carry this out two things are of utmost importance, they must be educated as to what are their political and civil rights, and they must learn the English language. This does not necessarily mean that the Mexican-Americans should forget their racial origin and their language. What these leaders propose to do is to arouse the political pride of these people by reminding them of their past traditions. The educated Mexican-American citizens realize the possibilities of their race and are fired by the desire to organize this element for the sole purpose of hastening the political development of their people.

For this purpose was created "The League of United Latin-American Citizens." This organization was inspired no doubt by the order of the "Sons of America," organized in San Antonio, in 1921 by James Tafolla, an attorney. The purpose of this league was to unite all citizens of Mexican or Spanish extraction.

Mexican-American citizens in the Río Grande Valley called a convention at Harlingen, Texas on August 24, 1927. The "Sons of America" as well as other civic organizations sent their representative. All the delegates, with the exception of those of the "Sons of America," wanted the organization of a new league, with the result that "The League of Latin American Citizens" was organized. Local councils have been established at McAllen, Encino del Pozo, Brownsville, and La Grulla.

Another convention was called on February 17, 1929, at Corpus Christi for the purpose of discussing a basis of union for all the organizations throughout Texas. Twenty-five delegates met, and the following proposals were made:

1. Adoption of the name "United Latin-American Citizens."
2. Membership to be confined to American citizens of Latin extraction.
3. Recognition of all local councils represented in the convention as councils of the new organization.
4. The establishment of English as the official language.
5. The adoption of a set of twenty-five fundamental principles.
6. The aims and purposes of the League as given below show the character of the organization:

The Aims and Purposes of This Organization Shall Be:
1. To develop within the members of our race the best, purest, and most perfect type of a true and loyal citizen of the United States of America.
2. To eradicate from our body politic all intents and tendencies to establish discriminations among our fellow citizens on account of race, religion, or social position as being contrary to the true spirit of Democracy, our Constitution and Laws.
3. To use all the legal means at our command to the end that all citizens in our country may enjoy equal rights, the equal protection of the laws of the land and equal opportunities and privileges.

4. The acquisition of the English language, which is the official language of our country, being necessary for the enjoyment of our rights and privileges, we declare it to be the official language of this organization, and we pledge ourselves to learn and speak and teach same to our children.

5. To define with absolute and unmistakable clearness our unquestionable loyalty to the ideals, principles, and citizenship of the United States of America.

6. To assume complete responsibility for the education of our children as to their rights and duties, and the language and customs of this country; the latter, in so far as they may be good customs.

7. We solemnly declare once and for all to maintain a sincere and respectful reverence for our racial origin of which we are proud.

8. Secretly and openly, by all lawful means at our command, we shall assist in the education and guidance of Latin-Americans and we shall protect and defend their lives and interest whenever necessary.

9. We shall destroy any attempt to create racial prejudice against our people, and any infamous stigma which may be cast upon them, and we shall demand for them the respect and prerogatives which the Constitution grants to us all.

10. Each of us considers himself with equal responsibilities in our organization, to which we voluntarily swear subordination and obedience.

11. We shall create a fund for our mutual protection, for the defense of those of us who may by unjustly persecuted and for the education and culture of our people.

12. This organization is not a political club, but as citizens we shall participate in all local, state, and national political contests. However, in doing so we shall ever bear in mind the general welfare of our people, and we disregard and abjure once and for all any personal obligation which is not in harmony with these principles.

13. With our vote and influence we shall endeavor to place

in public office men who show by their deeds, respect and consideration for our people.

14. We shall select as our leaders those among us who demonstrate, by their integrity and culture, that they are capable of guiding and directing us properly.

15. We shall maintain publicity means for the diffusion of these principles and for the expansion and consolidation of this organization.

16. We shall pay our poll tax as well as that of members of our families in order that we may enjoy our rights fully.

17. We shall define our ideals by means of the press, lectures, and pamphlets.

18. We shall oppose any radical and violent demonstration which may tend to create conflict and disturb the peace and tranquility of our country.

19. We shall have mutual respect for our religious views and we shall never refer to them in our institutions.

20. We shall encourage the creation of educational institutions for Latin-Americans and we shall lend our support to those already in existence.

21. We shall endeavor to secure equal representation for our people on juries and in the administration of governmental affairs.

22. We shall denounce every act of peonage and mistreatment a well as the employment of our minor children of scholastic age.

23. We shall resist and attack energetically all machinations tending to prevent our social and political unification.

24. We shall oppose any tendency to separate our children in the schools of this country.

25. We shall maintain statistics which will guide our people with respect to working and living conditions and agricultural and commercial activities in the various parts of our country.[9]

What the success of the League will be is to be seen. Those who have undertaken this movement are educated men, some self-made who because of their tenacity and persistency have risen above their class. Others are descendants of the old landed aristocracy. One thing is characteristic of all these men. They are politicians, and that is where the danger lies. Border politics are just emerging from political boss-ism and rings. If the League tends to educate the Mexican-Americans for purely altruistic reasons, its labor no doubt is meritorious and praiseworthy. But should county bossism be superseded by an organized state wide political machine, the results will be detrimental not only to the Mexican-American citizens but to the state at large.

Dr. Weeks of the University of Texas is more optimistic on the subject and makes the following conclusion:

> In conclusion, may it be said that educated Mexican-Americans in general as well as the members of the League of United Latin American Citizens, are agreed that the problem with which they and their racial brothers are faced in Texas and the United States have been created quite as much by their own deficiencies as by the deficiencies of the Anglo-American in his dealings with the two races and two civilizations. In order, therefore, that these people may be able to stand their ground, they must correct their own deficiencies, resulting from igno-rance, docility, and prejudice against the Anglo-Saxon and his ways, And doing such, they must show him that they can meet his standards and hence can demand his rights. Thus, without sacrificing the best of their racial heritage, they can remove his racial prejudice.[10]

CHAPTER 6

What the Coming
of the Americans Has Meant
to the Border People

The beginning of the century brought the Renaissance to the border counties. It was an awakening in every sense of the word, socially, politically, and economically. For nearly two hundred years the Texas-Mexicans had lived knowing very little and caring less of what was going on in the United States. They looked southward for all the necessities and pleasures in life. Mexican newspapers brought them news of the outside, their children were educated in Mexican schools, Spanish was the language of the people, Mexican currency was used altogether. When the women craved for finery, it was acquired across the river.

The counties in which these people lived were run by Mexicans, and everywhere, with the exception of Brownsville, the Americans were considered foreigners. These people had lived so long in their communities that it was home to them, and home to them meant Mexico. They lived happily ignorant that they were foreigners in a foreign land. As all provincial people, they considered themselves the elect of the community and looked down in disdain at the few Americans or Europeans who settled among them. The landed aristocracy, impregnable in their racial pride, lived in a world of their own sincerely believing in their rural greatness.

The few American families living in these communities had to adapt themselves to the existing conditions of the element among which they lived, and had become, as has been previously stated, Mexicanized. They spoke Spanish, a few had become Catholic, and many had intermarried with the Texas-Mexican element. The children from these unions had not in any way assimilated the customs and habits of the American parent, but had remained untouched and thoroughly Mexican.

Rude then, was the awakening of these border people when the development of the Río Grande Valley brought hundreds of foreigners to their doors. This invasion of fortune-seeking Americans was a material as well as a spiritual blow to the Mexicans, particularly to the landed aristocracy.

On the other hand, to the *jornaleros* or day laborers, this economic change improved their status in many respects. It meant more than a change of masters, it meant more work, better wages and improved living conditions. No class of society has gained as much by the economic changes as the *jornalero* class has. As previously stated, there has been a shifting of the day laborers from the ranches to the cities. And this has been a great step in the improvement of their condition. However hard their work may be in the towns, it is not as heavy as what they had to do on the ranches, and the wages are much better. Whereas they had earned fifty cents a day as farmhands or goatherds, they are now making anywhere from one dollar to two dollars per day. The old one room *jacal* has been replaced by a small lumber house for which they are paying on the installment plan. The laborers themselves are better dressed, they wear store-bought clothes and their wives may attain their highest ambition, wearing a hat.

They work in the truck garden plantations, in the orange and lemon groves. In the spring and summer they migrate to the fields, to chop or pick cotton as the case may be. During this season enough is earned by the whole family for the winter, should there be a scarcity of work. These people are content with their economic uplift and care very little or nothing as to the treatment they receive from their American masters. They do not resent any racial distinction or discrimination, the difference between them and their masters is no greater than that which separated them from their former *amos*.

The children of this class are doing something that their parents never accomplished; they are going to school, learning to read, to write, and to speak English. Altogether they are thoroughly satisfied with their lot.

Dissatisfaction, however, is rampant among the middle classes, composed of small shopkeepers and artisans. They read much, mostly in Spanish and they are the thinkers. It is from this group that the United League of Latin Americans gets its members. The laborers are too contented to want more, and the landowners are not interested in the League unless they can be the leaders. This middle class is receiving a public school education and the most ambitious of its members are working their way through institutions of high learning.

Economically both classes resent the invasion of the Americans. The introduction of new and improved methods, the chain stores, and Piggly Wigglies has driven the middle class grocers out of business. The same thing has happened with owners of dry goods stores, drug stores, etc.

It hurts the landowners' pride to see these foreigners do in a short time what they had not been able to accomplish in years. They have seen the Americans appropriate all that had been theirs, even the desert plains. The new arrivals bought this seemingly worthless land at a very low price, and by irrigation and modern machinery have converted the desert into a garden. An undercurrent of dissatisfaction is felt all over the country amongst these two classes. In the towns they see themselves segregated into their own quarters as an inferior race.

The friendly feeling which had slowly developed between the old American and Mexican families has been replaced by a feeling of hate, distrust, and jealousy on the part of the Mexicans. The descendants of the Americans who married Mexican wives in the middle nineteenth century are more Mexicanized than the Mexicans themselves, and some are even ashamed of their American blood.

All over the border counties, with the exception of such towns as Laredo, Rio Grande City, and Brownsville, where the Mexican element predominates, a contest between the two elements is being waged. It is a racial struggle, a fight between an aggressive, conquering and material people and a passive, volatile, but easily satisfied race. It is the struggle between the New World and the Old, for the Texas-Mexicans have retained more than their brethren in Mexico Old World traditions, customs, and ideals. The old families resent the gulf with which the newly arrived Americans have separated them. Not that they are anxious for the friendship of the American families but they object to the fact that they are considered an inferior race. The word *white*, which the Americans use to differentiate themselves from the Mexican population, is like a red flag to a bull.

In an interview which the writer had with a Roma citizen whose family had been in Texas for two hundred years the following was gathered:

> "We, Texas-Mexicans of the border," he said, "although we hold on to our traditions, and are proud of our race, are loyal to the United States, in spite of the treatment we receive by some of the new Americans. Before their arrival, there were no racial or social distinctions between us. Their children married ours, ours married theirs, and both were glad and proud of the fact. But since the coming of the 'white trash' from the north and middle west we felt the change. They made us feel for the first time that we were Mexicans and that they considered themselves our superiors.
>
> "In spite of these things we showed our loyalty during the World War when we sent our sons to the front, and when those of us who were too old to serve in the army offered our services free of charge to the Draughting Board and war commissions. We hoped that this would change the Americans' attitude toward us, but to them we are still Mexicans. We are told that the trouble lies in the fact that we keep to ourselves and do not want to assimilate. Some of us are willing to do that, but how can we when not for a moment are we allowed to forget the fact that we are Mexicans? That being the case, we are not going to thrust our society upon a people who do not want us. Instead

of becoming Americanized we are getting farther and farther away from that and are drawing ourselves within a shell of self-consciousness and racial pride."

In Edinburg, Hidalgo County, I interviewed a young married man, an official in the Court House, as to what he thought the solution to the interracial problem would be.

"That is a difficult problem to solve," said he, "we lived so long to ourselves as Mexicans, and looked upon Mexico as our country that it is hard for us to cope with the situation. We were wholly unprepared, politically, educationally, and socially when the avalanche of Americans fell upon us. The fact that we received an entirely Mexican education, I am a product of the Colegio Altamirano in Hebbronville, made it difficult for us to understand American ideals. And it is our place and our duty now to learn American ways, to send our children to American schools, to learn the English language, not that we are ashamed of our Mexican descent, but because these things will enable us to demand our rights and to improve ourselves. We understand our race, and when we are able to comprehend American ideas and ideals, American ways and customs, we shall be worth twice as much as they, and we certainly shall have the advantage over them. Americans are egoists, and provincial, they over estimate their power and doing so are unwilling to see any other way but their own, It is to our advantage then, to educate ourselves in American institutions, to learn the English language and to exercise our rights as citizens. My children are to receive a public education here, and when they graduate, I shall send them to Mexico for at least two years in order that they may perfect themselves in the Spanish language and that they may know Mexico as Mexico is. We are going now through a very painful period of transition and like the white black bird do not know yet just what we are. Mexicans from across the river look down upon us and call us by what to them is the vilest epithet, *Texanos* and the Americans do not consider us as such, although some of our Texas-Mexican families have lived here for generations.

"For years we have been part of a big political machine, our vote has not been individual, but now that we are becoming conscious of the meaning of citizenship we want to exert our privileges as individuals. Our labor is arduous, the future welfare of the Texas-Mexicans depends on what will be accomplished during this generation."

The farther one gets away from the river the worse conditions are. In the towns along the boundary line where the descendants of the old grantees live, they have more or less demanded certain privileges, which they still retain.

Segregation of the two races is practiced in every town north of the counties bordering the river. After the World War, when the boys returned from France, a fraternal spirit animated by a common bond made the Texas-Mexicans hope for a change. But this superficial outburst of enthusiasm and emotion was not lasting. Many incidents which occurred lately have disgusted the Texas-Mexicans to such an extent that some have changed from the most loyal American subjects to the bitterest anti-Americans.

Two years ago in Falfurrias, Brooks County, the American legion had a Fourth of July celebration and dance. For this purpose subscriptions were made from the merchants of the town both Mexican and American. On the day of the celebration all the boys wearing the Legion badges attended the barbecue. All went well. But in the evening when some of the Mexican boys wanted to dance, they were told that the dance was only for *whites*. This, as might well be imagined, was taken as an insult by the Mexican legionnaires. One of them, who had received a decoration for bravery, snatched it from his coat lapel, threw it on the floor and trampled it saying, "If shedding my blood for you Americans does not mean anymore than this, I do not want to ever wear your colors, from now on I am ashamed of having served in your army."

Both classes, the middle and the landowners, are thoroughly disgusted with the situation; the former aspires to the social equality it feels it must have, the second simply demands what it always had. They oppose the discrimination that is shown concerning their attending certain public places. They resent the fact that in some of the Valley towns, Mexicans are not admitted at cafes, picture shows, hotels, and bathing beaches. The Americans contend that they have been forced to use segregation because of the hundreds of day laborers that would swarm into these places if Mexicans were permitted. The Mexicans on the other hand argue that the laborers are used to segregation in their own country and would not attempt to attend places that the better element frequents. They claim that it would be equally as unfair for Europeans to classify an Anglo-American with an American Negro, as it is to consider a Spanish-Mexican the social equal of an Indian laborer. The Texas-Mexican families do not want social intercourse with Americans. But they do demand the privilege of attending the same public places as Americans do. They are very conservative, have kept the Spanish traditions in regard to the position of woman and look down upon American customs as free, loose, and immoral. Girls are not allowed the companionship of boys, and just seeing American boys and girls together is contaminating to the Mexican youth.

Mexican parents disapprove thoroughly of their children associating with Americans. According to their ethics, woman was made for the home, her duty in life is to create a home and to bring children into the world. In the freedom which American girls enjoy, parents see the beginning of all social evils. Sports are discouraged as tending to make woman masculine. When a Brownsville mother brought her daughter to one of the most exclusive girls' schools in San Antonio, her chief concern was that she should not play tennis because, "playing tennis tended to take away woman from the home."

"I am told that becoming Americanized means being progressive," said a leading Río Grande City citizen, "but if that means that my daughter will bob her hair, disobey her parents, chew gum, smoke, drink, and be out with boys until late at night, and finally elope, and get a divorce at the end of one or two years [of]married life, I do not want progress. That is just what American civilization means to us. Our customs may be of the old world, they suited our parents and they suit us now."

One cannot help but wonder at the last statement.

If the older generation feels that way about Americanization the young people do not. The fact that they are all rapidly learning English points in the opposite direction. Ten years ago when visiting the Valley it was noticed that a very small percentage of the school children spoke English. The penalty for using Spanish during recess hours was to make the culprits stand at the place where they were caught *in flagrante*. That order had to be suspended for not one Mexican child was able to play.

Last summer when in the same community, I was amazed to hear all the children, even those under scholastic age, speak English, and slang at that.

There is a group of advanced progressive Texas-Mexicans who, realizing that the future of their children depends upon their getting an American education are sending their sons and daughters to American colleges and universities. And when these girls are among typical American college girls they are not going to sit in their rooms and uphold family traditions. When in Rome they will do as the Romans do. All of these girls are in the process of receiving their education. What their reaction will be when they go back home after four or five years of complete freedom is yet to be seen. Many of the boys are studying the professions: law, medicine, pharmacy, engineering. When this crop of American educated young men return to their respective towns, will they submit to the racial distinctions prevalent in the border towns? That also is a future problem.

Young Texas-Mexicans are being educated. Behind them lies a store of traditions of another race, customs of past ages, an innate and inherited love and reverence for another country. Ahead of them lies a struggle of which they are to be the champions. It is a struggle for equality and justice before the law, for the just demands of full-fledged American citizens. They bring with them a broader view, a clearer understanding of the good and bad qualities of both races. They are the converging element of two antagonistic civilizations; they have the blood of one and have acquired the ideals of the other. They, let it be hoped, will bring to an end the racial feuds that have existed in the border for nearly a century.

Notes

CHAPTER 1

1. Herbert E. Bolton. *Texas in the Middle Eighteenth Century, Studies in Spanish Colonial History and Administration* (Berkeley: University of California Press, 1915), 288.

2. Ibid., 293.

3. Alejandro Prieto, *Historia de las Tamaulipas*, (México, 1873), 172–74.

4. Polly Pearl Crawford, The Beginnings of Spanish Settlements in the Lower Río Grande Valley, master's thesis, University of Texas, 1925.

5. México, *Archivo General de la Nación, Historia, Descripción General de la Nueva Colonia de Santander*, Tomo 55, p. 64, University of Texas Library.

6. *El Fronterizo* (Río Grande City), September 15, 1925.

7. México, *Archivo General de la Nación*. Tomo 55, p. 64, University of Texas Library.

8. Prieto, *Historia de las Tamaulipas*, 172–75.

9. Ibid., 207.

10. Ibid., 212.

11. Matamoros Archives, Vol. XIV, 150. Lucas Fernández to the border towns, 1827.

12. Matamoros Archives, Vol. XIII, 155.

13. México, *Archivo General de la Nación*. Tomo 55, p. 64.

14. México, *Archivo General de la Nación*. Tomo 55, p. 64.

15. Henderson K. Yoakum. *History of Texas from Its First Settlement in 1685 to Its Annexation to the United States in 1846* (New York: Redfield, 1856), 289.

16. Ibid.

17. Emilio del Castillo Negrete, *México en el Siglo XIX*, 141.

18. Letter from Gen. Antonio Canales to H.W. Haines. *Gaceta del Gobierno de Tamaulipas Ciudad Victoria*, November 28, 1840, 1.

19. Moses Austin, *The Austin Papers*, ed. Eugene Barker, Annual Report of the American Historical Association. v. 2, 1922.

20. *Comisión Pesquisidora de la Frontera del Norte*, 148–50.

21. J. Frank Dobie, *A Vaquero of the Brush Country* (Dallas, TX: Southwest Press, 1929), 50.

22. John S. Ford (Colonel), *Memoirs*, Vol. 4, p. 789, MS, University of Texas Library.

23. Personal interview with Juan Flores, Río Grande City, one of Cortina's men.

24. J. Frank Dobie, *A Vaquero of the Brush Country*, 53.

25. Major Heintzelman to Colonel Lee, Fort Brown, Texas, March 1, 1860. *Executive Documents*, First Session of the Thirty-Sixth Congress, 1859–60, p.6.

26. Major Heintzelman to Colonel Lee, Fort Brown, Texas, March 1, 1860. *Executive Documents*, First Session of the Thirty-Sixth Congress, 1859–60, p. 13.

CHAPTER 2

1. Escandón to the Viceroy, April 17, 1749, *Provincias Internas*, 179, 341.

2. "Inspección de Nuevo Santander," in *Archivo General de la Nación, Historia, Descripción General de La Nueva Colonia de Santander*, Tomo 55, Mexico City, 1757, p. 64.

3. Date carved on beam of first home built there.

4. F. C. Pierce, *Texas' Last Frontier*, 40.

5. *El Fronterizo* (Río Grande City) August 22, 1925. Titles from Monroe Abstract and Title Company, Río Grande City.

6. Family history of Don Francisco de la Garza Martínez, recorded in volume 49, pp. 308–12, Deed Records, Starr County, Texas.

7. Personal interview with Mrs. Rosa Davis Viscaya, daughter of Henry Clay Davis, Río Grande City, August 17, 1929.

8. *El Fronterizo* (Río Grande City) August 22, 1925.

9. Articles of agreement between Henry Clay Davis and First Lieutenant J. A. Alley, Third Infantry, A.A.Q. Master U.S. Army. In possession of Mrs. Rosa Davis Viscaya, Río Grande City.

10. *El Fronterizo* (Río Grande City), August 22, 1925.

11. F. C. Pierce, *Texas' Last Frontier*, 21.

12. Ibid., 41–42.

13. Ibid., 42, 43, 44.

14. Ibid., 47.

15. Ibid., 38–54.

16. Ibid., 81.

17. Ibid., 103.

18. Ibid.

19. Ibid., 108–11.

20. Ibid., 115.

CHAPTER 3

1. Data taken from the records in the Land Office in the Kleberg County Court House. August 25, 1929.

2. Material collected from the different county court houses on the border. Summer, 1929.

3. Data collected from the county clerk's office. Property Rolls of 1928. Summer, 1929.

CHAPTER 4

1. F. C. Pierce, *Texas' Last Frontier*, 122–35.

2. *Texas Almanac*, 1860, 125–26.

3. Unsigned letter, 1–6, Kingsbury Collection, University of Texas.

4. *A Sketch of Brownsville*, Kingsbury Collection, 1–6.

5. Pierce, *Texas' Last Frontier*, 125–27.

6. Dobie, *A Vaquero of the Brush Country*, 50. Don Francisco Guerra y Guerra who owned one of these trains operating between Saltillo and San Antonio in 1878 tells of the attacks that the cart drivers suffered at the hands of the Americans.

7. A *real* is a Mexican coin valued at twelve cents Mexican money, six *reales* is equivalent to about seventy-five cents Mexican currency [in 1929].

8. Reminiscences of Don Francisco Guerra y Guerra, ranchman, politician, descendant of Don Francisco Guerra, surveyor of the grants for Mier in 1768. Now deceased, lived 98 years; 78 years in Texas. August 20, 1929; personal interview with Doña Isabel Garcia, at San Diego, Texas. August 25, 1929; personal interview with Doña Domasita Cisneros de Canales, descendant of Juan Nepomuceno Cortina; personal interview with Mrs. Dolores Guerra de Treviño, now 65, who witnessed many dances and St. John's celebrations at her father's ranch, Las Viboras, in Starr County.

9. Testament of Don José Vásquez Borrego, in possession of Mrs. Darío Sánchez, Laredo, Texas.

10. Interview with Don Domingo Reyna, at las Cuevitas ranch, Jim Hogg County.

11. An old lady whose four grandsons fought in the World War told me the following story: "I did not want to marry Ricardo because his face was always red. When his father asked mine for my hand I refused him on that ground. 'My daughter,' said my father severely, 'You do not want him for an ornament, but for a husband.' And so I married him."

12. W. H. Chatfield, *The Twin Cities of the Border* (New Orleans: Brandao, 1893) 3.

13. Reminiscences of Miss Antoinette Stewart, aged 80 years. Río Grande City, Starr County, Texas, August 17, 1929.

14. This material was collected from several old people who lived through this period and remember conditions as they existed some fifty years back, and who have witnessed the development of the country. Such are Miss Katie Edwards, now in Edinburg, seventy-five years old, who lived at Río Grande City and Roma, Miss Florentina Cox living at Roma, Don Francisco Guerra y Guerra, a ranchman in Starr county, Mrs. Rosa Davis Viscaya, Río Grande City.

15. Don Manuel Guerra.

16. *Revista Católica*, Las Vegas, New Mexico, September 19, 1915.

17. From Dolores Corréa Zapata, *La Mujer en el Hogar.* This text was in use in 1900 at a private school in the San Roman Ranch.

18. José Antonio Sanchez de la Barquera, *Compendio de Urbanidad, en verso,* 16–17, 21–22, 26.

19. *El Nacional,* Piedras Negras (Coahuila), July 7, 1927.

20. W. H. Chatfield, *The Twin Cities of the Border,* 10–11.

21. Ibid., 16.

22. This was practiced all over the border, several of my own relatives held certificates in this manner. It is from them that I have gathered this information.

23. Thomas Stewart, Miss Antoinette Stewart, Miss Lou Davis, Downy Davis, Pedro Nix, Miss Mamie Nix, Sam P. Vale, and José Vale.

24. School Reports. In the State Department of Education, for the scholastic years 1914–15, Austin, Texas.

CHAPTER 5

1. Statistics of population of the United States Tenth Census 1880. United States Census Report 1910, 804.

2. O. Douglas Weeks, "The League of United Latin American Citizens." Reprinted from *The Southwestern Political and Social Science Quarterly.* Vol. 10, No. 3, December, 1929, Austin, 8–11.

3. Testimony of James B. Wells, Glasscock and Parr. Supplement to the Senate Journal, Regular Session of the 36th Legislature (Texas 1919, Austin), 846–51.

4. Ibid., 890.

5. Family records in my possession taken from the Mier archives, supplemented by archives in possession of Don Luis García Mier, Tamaulipas, Mexico.

6. *Corona Funebre, Dedicada a honrar la amada memoria de Don Manuel Guerra,* Río Grande City, Texas, June 9, 1915, 2–6.

7. *Brownsville Herald*, (Brownsville, Texas), September 25, 1928. Written by Miss Celia Perez, Río Grande City, Texas. This is the essay verbatim as it appeared in the Brownsville paper. Miss Perez, daughter of a Republican leader in Río Grande City, had a Spanish education, therefore the mistakes in English.

8. O. Douglass Weeks, "The League of United Latin American Citizens." Reprinted from *The Southwestern Political and Social Science Quarterly*. Volume 10, Number 3, December 1929, Austin, Texas, 2.

9. Ibid., 8–10.

10. Ibid., 21–22.

Bibliography

[When possible formatting of bibliographic sources has been modified to conform to current editorial standards]

PRIMARY SOURCES
Manuscripts

Archivo General de la Nación. Historia, Descripción General de la Nueva Colonia de Santander, Tomo 55. Mexico City, 1757. University of Texas Library.

Austin, Moses, "The Austin Papers." Vol. 2, *Annual Report of the American Historical Association,* edited by Eugene Barker. 1922.

Borrego, Don José Vásquez. Testament in possession of Mrs. Darío Sánchez, Laredo, Texas. Cameron County. Court House. Summer 1929.

Canales, Antonio. Gen. Antonio Canales to H. W. Haines, November 28, 1840. In *Gaceta del Gobierno de Tamaulipas Ciudad Victoria.*

Comisión Pesquisadora de la Frontera del Norte, 1873.

(Report of the Committee of Investigation sent in 1873 by the Mexican government to the Frontier of Texas.)

Crawford, Pearl Polly. "The Beginnings of Spanish Settlements in the Lower Rio Grande Valley." Master's thesis, University of Texas, 1925.

Duval County. County Clerk. Property Rolls of 1928. Summer, 1929.

Ford, John S. (Colonel). *Memoirs.* University of Texas Library.

Jim Hogg County. County Clerk. Property Rolls of 1928. Summer, 1929.

Kingsbury, D. G. A collection of letters, sketches, and other material. University of Texas Library.

Kleberg County Court House. Land Office records. August 25, 1929.

Matamoros Archives, Vols. XIII–XIV.

Provincias Internas. University of Texas Library.

Starr County. Court House. Summer, 1929.

Texas Senate. Supplement to the Senate Journal, Regular Session, Thirty Sixth Legislature of Texas, 1919, Austin.

Texas State Dept. of Education. School Reports. 1914–15.

U.S. Census Office. Census Report, 1910.

U.S. Census Office. Tenth Census. 1880.

U.S. Congress. Executive Documents, First Session, Thirty Sixth Congress, 1859–60.

Weeks, Douglas O. "The League of United Latin American Citizens." Reprinted from *The Southwestern Political and Social Science Quarterly* 10, no. 3 (December, 1929).

Zapata County. County Clerk. Property Rolls of 1928. Summer, 1929.

Zapata County. Court House. Summer, 1929.

SECONDARY SOURCES

Bolton, Herbert E. *Texas in the Middle Eighteenth Century, Studies in Spanish Colonial History and Administration.* Berkeley: University of California Press, 1915.

Chatfield, W. H. *The Twin Cities of the Border.* New Orleans: Brandao, 1893.

del Castillo Negrete, Emilio. *México en el Siglo XIX.*

Dobie, J. Frank. *A Vaquero of the Brush Country.* Dallas, Tex: Southwest Press, 1929.

Pierce, Frank Cushman. *Texas' Last Frontier: A Brief History of the Lower Rio Grande Valley.* Menasha, Wis.: George Banta, 1917.

Prieto, Alejandro. *Historia de las Tamaulipas,* México, 1873.

Sanchez, José Antonio de la Barquera. *Compendio de Urbanidad, en verso.*

Texas Almanac. 1860; repr. 1928.

Yoakum, Henderson K. *History of Texas from Its First Settlement in 1685 to Its Annexation to the United States in 1846.* New York: Redfield, 1856.

Brownsville Herald (Brownsville, Texas). September 25, 1928.

El Fronterizo (Río Grande City, Texas). August 22, 1925, September 15, 1925.

El Nacional (Piedras Negras, Coahuila). July 7, 1927.

Gaceta del Gobierno de Tamaulipas (Ciudad Victoria). November 28, 1840, Matamoros Archives, University of Texas Library.

Revista Católica (Las Vegas, New Mexico). September 19, 1915.

Index

Paredes, Américo, 20–21, 22, 23
péons, 21–22, 76–80
Perez family, Duval County, 70
Petronila ranch, 49
Plan de San Diego, 30–31*n*8, 57–58
Point Isabel, Texas, 74
politics, border: as Anglo
  machinations, 18–19; Anglo-
  Mexican tradition differences, 96–
  97; bossism years, 97–100, 103–104;
  LULAC's creation, 26–28, 104–108;
  sheriff's elections, 100–103
population statistics, 96
Powers, Stephen, 97
Presbyterian school, 93
priests, 85–87
property owners. *See* landowners
Publications of the Texas Folklore Society (PTFS), 14–15

race relations: and Americanization
  process, 25–26, 113–16; in border
  conflicts, 51–58; Buffalo Soldiers
  conflict, 63; and folklore studies,
  13–14; LULAC formation, 104–108;
  Plan de San Diego, 30–31*n*8, 57–58;
  schooling ideals, 88–91, 93. *See also*
  immigrants, Anglo
railroads, 7–8, 9, 62, 73, 74–75
Ramirez, Angela, 91–92
Ramirez family, Starr County, 70
ranching lifestyle: Anglo
  immigration impact, 9, 12–13,
  24–25; colonization period, 48–49;
  landowner's, 80–83; and Texas
  independence, 51–52; worker-
  landowner relationship, 75–80
religion, 78, 85–87
Rentfro, R. B., 100–101
Republican Party, 100–103
Resaca de la Palma, 62, 64
Revilla, Texas, 48, 51

rhetoric of dominance, 4–6, 12–13,
  28–29
Río Grande City, Texas: class
  structure, 71; González's teaching,
  10; political leadership, 104;
  schools, 94; settlement history,
  49, 61–63, 65; social life, 83–85;
  transportation networks, 74
Río Grande republic, 53–54
Roma, Texas, 61, 71
Rotge, Domingo, 69
Rubottom, E. J., 63

Saenz, Juan Angel, 61
Salinas, Juan, 61
San Antonio, Texas, 9–11
Sánchez, Tomas, 50
San Ignacio, Texas, 60
San Jacinto battle, 53
San Jose ranch, 55–56
Santa Ana, 53
Saunders, John, 73
Sayers, Joseph, 63
schooling. *See* education
settlement/colonization period, 17, 18,
  47–51
sheep shearing, 80, 81
Shely, W. W., 100, 101, 102
sheriff's elections, 100–103
singing/music, 78–79, 80, 83–84
Sons of America, 104–105
Spain, 18, 47–51
Spanish-American War, 63
St. John's Day, 79
St. Joseph's school, 92–93
Staples, Stephen, 73
steamboats, 73–74
storytelling, 80

Tafolla, James, 104
Tamaulipas, Texas, 63–64
Tampico, Texas, 61